There is a tide in the affairs of men,

Which, taken at the flood, leads on to fortune;

Omitted, all the voyage of their life

Is bound in shallows and in miseries.

On such a full sea are we now afloat

And we must take the current when it serves,

Or lose our ventures.

William Shakespeare

NICHOLAS MORANT'S

Canada

by
J.F. Garden

FOOTPRINT
PUBLISHING CO. LTD.

Title page: The Larch trees are in fall glory along the Great Divide at Eohippus Lake in British Columbia. To the south, Mt.Assiniboine peers around the shoulder of Nestor Peak. At the right is the shadowed north face of The Monarch. Eohippus Lake is named after ancient horse fossils (Eohippus, the "dawn horse") found near this sight. These dog sized creatures first evolved in North America but became extinct during the ice ages. With Spanish exploration of North America, the European horse was brought back in the 16th century and finally reached the northern plains tribes in the early 1700s. *NMC*

Contents page (page 6): The Peace Tower at the Parliament buildings in Ottawa is framed by the Gothic arches of the entranceway to the East Block. *NMC*

At right: The Banff-Jasper Icefields Highway was nothing more than a gravel road in the late summer of 1949. Nick has stopped his 1948 Chrysler above the Sunwapta River to make this photograph and the view looks south to Mt.Athabasca (11452') and the Athabasca Glacier, part of the Columbia Icefields. *NMC*

This book is dedicated to Nick Morant's friends, who are many, but particularly to Colin Haworth, whose stories and anecdotes were invaluable. Furthermore, it is especially dedicated to Willie and Nick, and to Betty.

Canadian Cataloguing in Publication Data

Garden, J.F.(John Franklin), 1948-
Nicholas Morant's Canada

ISBN 0-9691621-6-2

1.Morant, Nicholas, 1910-
2.Photographers—Canada—Biography.

3.Canadian Pacific Railway Company — Biography. 4.CPRail—Biography. 5.Canada—History—Pictorial works. 6. Canadian Pacific Railway Company— History—Pictorial works. 7.CP Rail— History—Pictorial works. I.Title
HE2810.C2G37 1998   779'.997106'092
C97-911115-3

Copyright: Nicholas Morant. NMC
             Canadian Pacific Corporate
             Archives. CPCA
             John F. Garden 1998

Printed in Canada by Friesen Printing,
Altona Manitoba
Typeset by Econolith Press
Layout and design by J.F.Garden

Distributed by Sandhill Book Marketing Ltd.

1-800-667-3848

Published by Footprint Publishing Co. Ltd.
Box 1830
Revelstoke, British Columbia, V0E 2S0

CONTENTS

Nick and Willie at Massive, Alberta, photographing
CPR passenger trains in fresh snow on a warm winter day,
circa, 1939. *NMC*

FOREWORD
by
Margaret Elizabeth Morant

I have in my possession a letter of sympathy written to my mother on the occasion of my father's death, recalling an unusual afternoon tea in the clubhouse on the Banff Springs Hotel golf course, at which my father and a friend were joined by Nicholas and "Willie" Morant, and the Social Hostess, Jeannie Alexander. It was a thoughtful, kindly letter, written by just such a man, a longtime friend of my family.

Some nine years later, I had occasion to express our sympathy to Nick in the loss of his beloved Ivy ("Willie"), and in his acknowledgment, received a warm invitation to tea in Banff.

Sometime later, my sister, her husband and I were held spellbound for an afternoon, as we were regaled with story after story from the wealth of experiences in Nick's chosen field.

From Peru to Greenland, from Alaska to a munitions freighter on the North Atlantic in wartime winter, Nick's cameras recorded an era in Canadian history unparalleled in its diversity of subject and theme. In 1963 Toronto Saturday Night voted Nick to be "Canada's most versatile photographer."

Other comments drawn from periodicals during the fifty-one-year span as Special Photographer for CP Limited, the holding company for CP Rail, are as follows:

"Besides `Millions' of newspapers, magazines, books and other literature, Nick's photos have adorned Canadian postage stamps, tens and one hundred dollar bills. We regard him as Canada's top rail photographer, but he also travels as liaison officer with T.V. units, and is given assignments to assist visiting camera men and journalists from all over the world."

Freeman Hubbard,
Railroad Magazine 1972

"He is probably the most widely published photographer in Canada, and although few people know his name, his pictures have been seen by more people, in more countries, than any other photographer. A consummate and highly entertaining storyteller."

Andy Zeilinski
Canadian Photography July 1979

"This alchemy of Nature (Emerald Lake) seems to capture precisely the alchemist's skill of this wise young-old photographer, who moves across that line between Commercial Photography and Fine Art as if it were not there at all."

Michael Asti-Rose
Western Living December 1981

In September of 1939, Nick Morant was severely injured in an encounter with a grizzly bear, having gone to the rescue of his companion, who had not reached safety as Nick had. These injuries required a nine-month recovery period, after which he tried to enlist in the Navy, but was firmly rejected.

He was, however, assigned to special duties by the Dominion Government in 1940, as Chief Photographer in the Department of Public Information, then to the Wartime Information Board, which latterly became the Stills Branch of the National Film Board. Nick Morant's five-year wartime service ended at the First United Nation's Conference in San Francisco in 1945. His recorded story of Canada's War effort on land, in the air, and on the Atlantic is unique and memorable.

Following the war years, Nick continued to receive acclaim for his photographic art, and for twelve years gave a series of pictorial presentations, ably assisted by Ivy, which correlated Art in Nature with selected music. These immensely popular "Talks Without Words" were given in the National Museum of Canada, Hart House, McGill University, and in Rochester, N.Y., and Daytona Beach, as well as in many groups and clubs across the Continent. Of these talks, Photo Age states that "the second half is a stopper. Color, plus sound become an experience. Nick Morant is superb. He is revealed for what he is, — a master of his medium, and one of Canada's most sensitive photographic artists."

Photo-Age July 1963

The National Geographic Society chose to honor Nick by including one of his photographs in their Centennial Issue, Odyssey, in 1988, the only Canadian thus represented. Possibly some of the reasons for these accolades lies in Nick's own words — *I always tried for the hard shot. What have you got to lose? A few frames, and your time. If it works, you get something wonderful.*

The culmination of a lifetime of unremitting effort in the pursuit of excellence was seen on October 24, 1990, when Nick was awarded Membership in the Order of Canada.

And what of the man? In January, 1990, the writer and Nicholas Morant were quietly wed, and it has been a delightful journey with one of the most considerate, humorous, and talented human beings — a man of complete integrity. Moreover, a nephew has observed that "Nick's interest in people is reflected in his photography."

It has been a pleasure to share visits and reminiscences with our friend and author John Garden, without whose interest and unceasing efforts these books would not have been brought into being.

Seven good years have preceded three years of sadness, in which Nick's health has been impaired by the onset of Alzheimer's disease. His courageous struggle has been typical of his lifelong approach to difficult situations, but alas, no one has yet been the victor in this most insidious affliction.

I count it a privilege to have shared some of the crowning years of the illustrious and highly regarded Nicholas Everard Morant.

Margaret Elizabeth Morant
January 10, 1998

NICHOLAS MORANT-PHOTOGRAPHER

Golfers play by Nick Morant, perched atop his legendary scaffold, as he sets up for a Banff Springs publicity photograph, circa 1954. *NMC*

Two photos at right: Morant engaged Tommy Tweed and Jacob Two Young Man, along with two young, scantily clad ladies, to carry out a spoof on golfing. The photographs found their way into the Company magazine, The Spanner, for the amusement of CPR employees. *NMC*

The Fairmont motorcar popped and backfired its way along the rails, winding past the rock bluffs that skirt the north shore of Lake Superior. The sound echoed violently off the granite walls, ceasing momentarily as the "speeder" passed through Red Sucker Tunnel. The sun, rising above a scud of clouds that seemed to touch the whitecaps driven before the cold fall wind, radiated warm light on the ancient granite cliffs.

Performing the daily track inspection, the assistant roadmaster clattered around the corner into Mink Cove, ten miles east of Marathon, Ontario. The canvas sides of his motorcar flapped in the breeze; spray flecked the windshield, thrown up by the waves breaking on the rugged shoreline only feet below the tracks. Glancing at his timecard, he pulled the throttle wide open. Train No.1 was due out of Marathon in a matter of minutes. He had to get on over to Coldwell to clear the passenger or he might find himself courting disaster.

Curving left through a cut and fill that led around to Mink Tunnel, the assistant roadmaster caught a glimpse of a sight that provoked a second look. There, upon the top of the cut, perched in the wind and the spray, was a collection of wooden tripods supporting an elaborate array of cameras, and standing there, a very cold looking soul huddled under a slicker.

A few days later, at the other end of the country, three golfers, stealing away from a convention meeting in the Banff Springs Hotel, were midway down the eighth fairway when they came across what appeared to be a house under construction, very close to the green. The framework of newly cut lumber was easily discernable and lay directly between them and the flagged hole. Moving closer, they saw that four players already occupied the green, that the framework was not a house but a scaffold about twenty-five feet high. Atop - a photographer with a large camera shouted instructions to the foursome below.

On another occasion at the same golf course, two disciples of the Royal and Ancient Game, registered at the clubhouse as coming from Savannah, Georgia, encountered a very strange pair on the second green. They wore somewhat strange haberdashery. One had the regalia of an Indian Chief with full war paint and a fine set of eagle feathers. He stood there arguing

In response to Morant, the British delegation to the
United Nations Conference of 1945 poses at the table. The
gentleman on the left is unidentified, but the others are,
British Prime Minister Clement Atlee, second from the left,
Anthony Eden, next to him, and Lord Halifax on the right.
NMC

with his partner - apparently over the "lie" of the ball. The second golfer had a suit of armour reminiscent of the days of the legendary Court of King Arthur. When the Indian delivered a crushing blow to the Knight's helmet with a mid-iron settling the argument, the visitors hastily decided to play around the hole. The last the two Georgians saw of the affair, the caddies, two young ladies in scanty costumes, attempted to render first aid to the fallen knight with the assistance of a pair of tinsmith shears, an oil can and a blowtorch.

Then, a scene at the First Meeting of the United Nations in San Francisco. A photo session was in progress in the British headquarters. For a full hour the Englishmen had suffered at the hands of the press. As the session began to wind down, a still photographer came forward and asked if he might take a shot of the three principals . . . Lord Halifax, Anthony Eden, and the British Prime Minister, Clement Atlee. The three obliged by sitting down together at the table. But the photographer wasn't satisfied! *"Mr. Eden,"* he said quietly, *"Would you be so kind as to open your briefcase and pull out some papers so that you'll look as if you're working?"* The delegates laughed heartily. Then Anthony Eden replied in the diplomatic manner for which he was famous. "That's the first damned constructive suggestion we've had this morning!"

Mr.Eden did not know the photographer who so brashly approached him back in 1945. Nor did the golfers who avoided his scaffold, or played around his unlikely characters on the back nine. Nor did most of his fellow employees in the early days. Only his employers at Canadian Pacific knew of him, and then even they were not always sure what he did!

Now his name is widely recognized. Nicholas Everard Morant had the distinction of serving a career as "Special Photographer" assigned to the Public Relations Department of the Canadian Pacific Railway. He became a part of the van of Canadian photographers that included Harry Rowed, Yousuf Karsh, and Louis and Ronnie Jaques. Though not as prolific as some, nor as widely recognized, since most of his work bore the byline, "photo - Canadian Pacific," critics recognized him as the most versatile. His role was to portray Canadian Pacific, its entities and affiliates,

Some of the publications to which Nicholas Morant's Photographs were put to use.   NMC

Page 14 and 15: On location at Lake Louise, Nick and Willie prepare the models for a shoot. Morant has his 8 x 10 Deardorf on the tripod. *NMC*

Above: High on Mt.Fidelity in the Selkirk Mountains of British Columbia, (at the National Research Council's Avalanche Research Station) Willie made this photograph of Nick with his 4 x 5 Speed Graphic, circa 1963. *NMC*

At right: Looking eastward up the Illecillewaet Valley toward Roger's Pass, Willie made this photograph of Nick's silhouette at Mt.Fidelity. The Sir Donald Range dominates the horizon with Avalanche Mountain (9397') on the left, then Eagle Peak (9363'), Uto Peak (9620'), and Mt.Sir Donald (Syndicate Peak) (10,818') on the right. The Trans-Canada Highway stands out with its newly paved black asphalt surface winding up the valley. When early railway surveyors ventured up this valley all they could see was an impassable wall of peaks. Major A.B. Rogers, hired by the CPR to find a pass through the Selkirks, bushwacked up the Illecillewaet

from the Columbia with his nephew and native guides. When they reached the wall of peaks that we see in this photograph in September 1881, they climbed the alder and snow choked slopes of Avalanche Mountain to see if they could see any outlet from the valley. They discovered that a small tributary of the Illecillewaet River flowed southward from an alpine valley (to the left in the photograph) that might offer passage to the east. Because of the lateness of the season, it remained until the summer of 1882 before Rogers could prove that the pass existed. *NMC*

in a manner becoming the nation, and to attract customers and promote services. In the process, his photographs became a part of Canadiana, circulating on dollar bills and stamps. Morant photographs appeared on covers and in the pages of Life, The Star Weekly, Sports Afield, The New York Daily Mirror, The London Times, Fortune and Readers Digest, to name a few. He and his wife, "Willie," became ambassadors at large for both the CPR and Canada as they toured North America presenting their photographic lecture, "A Talk Without Words." They met many, many people. Most of them did not forget the Morants.

From the days of his youth in the frontier town of Kamloops, British Columbia, to the editorial rooms of the Winnipeg Free Press and the corporate halls of CP's Windsor Station, to the not-so-quiet

days of retirement in Banff, Alberta, Morant's work provides a glimpse of Canada in an age of development. He has photographed Canada's people, Canada's landscape and Canada's endeavors in peace and war. He has quietly guided top level Hollywood directors and their petulant actors through many a difficult movie scene on location on CP property. Yet for all that he did, his reputation exists principally among those with whom he has dealt through the long years.

Morant stems from a lineage that mixed culture and venture in balanced quantities. His mother was a poetess; his father a soldier - rancher, both exploring new life and new difficulties in a new land.

His creed respects fellow humans as equals, without regard to race, religion, or social position. Thus he adapts to any

milieu. He is as comfortable and effective in a corporate board room as in a shack alongside a mountain railway or in an auditorium jam-packed with spectators. This savoir-faire quality has served him well; it has also served those who have met with him.

He is a perfectionist in preparing for and shooting a picture, in processing film, in making prints, in quickly boiling up a pot of tea on the stove or in the wilderness. He has lived with a personal gospel of perfection, sometimes to the annoyance of bosses and friends who do not understand his obsessive compulsion to do things properly. He can be a bitter pill at times!

The high quality of his work has been due in great measure to this persistence. A near prima-donna approach does not usually go over in the business world.

Morant reasoned that his "superiors" would accept his manner if the product proved faultless. He has a secure sense of self-worth, so has never felt the need to become belligerent or to "strong-arm" anyone. Patiently he would use common sense to argue or gently explain a point. Given a standoff he was not averse to doing a job both ways, the results usually proving his the correct course.

Nick will claim all this is nonsense. Nonsense to him perhaps, but he is not that introspective. Nick Morant is very humble, but practical.

Nor is Morant a split personality case, but consciously or unconsciously, he plays out one of two roles as befits the occasion. His roots (try to get him to admit it) are from the better side of British landed gentry who lived in late 19th century elegance, on a first name basis with distinguished Britons including, for example, the Poet-Laureate John Masefield. This familiarity with gentility, even a generation removed, remained. It accounts for the ease with which Morant could face a boardroom full of tycoons, or Royalty, with nary a tremor. Other than bank balances, individual principles and moral character, they were, in a way, equal.

The other role is that of a perfectionist in whatever he undertakes. It does not come from his family background as much as from some inherent sense that "things" must be done right. He is uncomfortable if his sense of perfection does not prevail. Take comfort; he has always treated senior executives this way.

Then there was (and still is) the Morant of the newsroom. His traits are horseplay and nonsense, colorful language, and the frankly expressed detestation of children. He is credited for many nicknames attached to both familiar and distant acquaintances. His letters to friends are commonly addressed "Dear Sam," and even his dear wife gained the nickname "Willie." He is without doubt an irreverent jokester.

Willie photographed Nick at work (opposite page) making the publicity photograph we see on this page of the dining room in the Chateau Lake Louise. The prominent mountain with the ice hanging from the top is Mt.Lefroy (11,230'), named by Sir James Hector of the Palliser Expedition after General Sir John Henry Lefroy (1817-1890), a noted astronomer and head of the Toronto Observatory from 1842-1853. Both photos NMC

Fort Henry, built in 1813, is part of the Royal Military College in Kingston, Ontario and overlooks Kingston Harbour at the eastern end of Lake Ontario. Each day in the summer season cadets put on military displays and exercises. In the picture above Willie used her 35mm Leica camera to capture Nick and his assistant as they prepared to make a photograph (at left) of the gun crews swinging their artillery piece into position for firing atop the parapet of Fort Henry. Both photos *NMC*.

Morant has never taken the stance of a public personality. Nor has he posed as an heroic figure. Yet his behavior towards his guide during the disaster with a grizzly bear is as shining an example of the "reluctant hero" theme as one is likely to encounter outside the theater.

His long relationship with his late wife, Ivy Young of Winnipeg, was a working partnership of great strength and uncommon viability. The affection was not a matter for public display, but during the war, as he was about to take his cameras to sea in a freighter full of high explosives and munitions, he sent a note to his closest friend from what he referred to in the secrecy of wartime as "an Eastern Canada seaport." The note acknowledged a logical fear, but only in the form of a request that should anything happen, Ivy should be cared for.

Pages 22-23: Another of Willie's photographs presents a panorama of the Selkirk Mountains with Nick standing on the slopes of Fidelity Mountain, preparing to make a photograph on his Speed Graphic camera. *NMC*

On the Ross Lake trail in Yoho National Park, British Columbia, Morant pauses with his pack load of camera gear as Willie made this photograph in August, 1945. Down below is the old gravel road from Lake Louise to Golden that is now the Trans-Canada Highway, and a westbound freight descending the Big Hill down to Field. In the background is Mt.Field (8655') at left and Mt.Wapta (9116'), right, above the Yoho Valley. *NMC*

Perched high atop Sulphur Mountain above the Banff Springs Hotel, Nick was preparing a publicity shot on the 8x10 Deardorf when a Whiskey Jack (Gray jay or "camp robber") landed on his head in search of a tidbit. Willie, always nearby with her trusty Leica, alertly made the photograph before the bird realized that this was no picnic. NMC

The backwater ponds and beaver dams along the Bow River between Banff and Lake Louise afford some of the finest trout fishing anywhere. Such activities Morant publicized in an effort to attract clientele to the CPR's mountain hotels, and fishing is one of the most popular pastimes in the world. The magnificent scenery in the background does nothing to discourage visitors. Castle Mountain (9128') was named by Sir James Hector of the Palliser Expedition in 1857, renamed Mt.Eisenhower by the MacKenzie-King government in 1946 to honour General Dwight D. Eisenhower, Supreme Commander of Allied Forces in Europe during the Second World War, and changed back to the original name in 1979 due to public pressure. *NMC*

His concern for her and for others, for unfortunate children, aged and ailing neighbors, or a friend in financial straits, usually disguised under a raucous conversational screen of embarrassment, has a flavor of humanity that is sometimes missing in others who have had the satisfaction of success. It strikes me as a quality we would all like to call Canadian.

Laughter, unique in humans, takes the sharp edge off the solemn side of life. While always resolute in his work, or in the face of life's troubles, things are never so bad as to preclude some light-hearted fun in a Morant day. Life for Nick is never taken too seriously, his good nature bringing warmth to his life and those fortunate enough to know him.

In a very precarious position along the Spray River, Morant has set up his camera and tripod for a photograph of the canyon. Willie, ever his assistant, has helped bring the gear down and made this photograph on her Leica, circa 1945. *NMC*

While setting up for a pastoral scene in Nova Scotia, Morant ran into a slight problem. As cows will do, curiosity brought them across the field to investigate, and this one decided to discover whether this object was a new kind of salt block, or something else that might excite the taste buds. Willie Morant photo. *NMC*

At right: Using the Leica, Nick made a photograph of Willie with a Rollei around her neck, chatting with a native lady on Mayne Island, in the Gulf Islands. Morant owned many and various cameras of different formats during his career, all purchased personally. He claims he still has all but one, including a model called a Bildschite, the pieces of which now reside in a jar! *NMC*

On vacation from the <u>Winnipeg Free Press</u> in the summer of 1935, Morant spent time at the Stoney Creek bridge and photographed CPR's experimental 2-10-4 steam locomotive, No.8000. The camera he has is a 2 1/2 x 3 1/2 Contessa-Nettle that suffered serious focusing problems due to a poor shutter. He quickly sold this camera on his return to Winnipeg, and it became the only one to disappear from his collection. Nick and Willie were not yet married at the time this photograph was made, so the photographer is unknown, unless of course it is a self portrait. *NMC*

Part I

The Early Years

Nick Morant's father Francis was born of English aristocracy. His grandfather was Edward Morant, the lord and master of Roydon Manor, pictured here, a part of the Morant estate of Brockenhurst Park. Only once did Nick take any sort of vacation from his work at the CPR, and that was during 1967 when he and Willie crossed the Atlantic to visit the Morants of England. It was during that trip that Willie made this image of Nick setting up for a photograph of the manor. *NMC*

CHAPTER ONE
Life in a Frontier Town

Kamloops was a small settlement of 4,000 people at the confluence of the North and South Thompson Rivers when Francis George Morant arrived in the early 1900's. A veteran of South Africa's Boer War, and a keen outdoorsman, Morant came to Canada in search of wilderness adventure and a better life than his native England could offer. Many British immigrants and remittance men were settling the Okanagan and Thompson country during this period of history, encouraged by the Canadian Pacific Railway and the Canadian Government to homestead or bring their businesses to the Canadian West.

The Morant family, at one time titled, and wealthy landlords of thousand acre Brockenhurst estate near Southampton, had declined in prominence, allowing little room for a headstrong young soldier who ran afoul of his father. A measure of their relationship can be seen by the token inheritance of some £50 received in later years. Francis had no choice but to seek new horizons and a better life in a less regulated environment.

Subsequent to the purchase of a small fruit farm and house on the north shore of the Thompson River, Francis Morant sent back to England for his bride-to-be, Mary Catherine Edith Wylde ("Mollie" as she was familiarly known). She was a gentlewoman of proper upbringing, and an accomplished horse woman to boot. Her father, Everard William Wilde was a long-time official of the British Foreign Office. Like his daughter he too loved the horses, but in a manner that financially distressed his family. When Francis Morant came into her life, Mary Wylde did not hesitate to throw in her lot in with him. She felt compelled to relieve her family of some of the financial burden, to strike off from home with the man she loved.

The difficulties and hardships she encountered living in Kamloops tested her. Early in her marriage she returned to England on several occasions, her home in Kamloops lacking amenities that we accept as normal, such as hot and cold running water. Loneliness and the lack of social contact induced depression; she had to be self-reliant when her husband left on his game warden's duties, often for a month at a time. On June 29, 1910, her life changed forever, loneliness a thing of the past. Her first child, Nicholas Everard Morant was born. No doubt this event kept Mollie extremely busy because of their rudimentary lifestyle.

The fruit farm was a lovely and exciting place for a child to grow up on. Mollie's love of animals carried over to her son; they were his first playmates and companions. The unsettled country back of the farm gave room for a young fellow to grow up with dogs and cats, horses and cattle; and Indians yet roamed through the territory.

Kamloops sits in a semi-desert landscape with sagebrush and tumbleweed, Ponderosa Pines, and rattlesnakes searching for shade in the 90 degree Fahrenheit weather common in summer. The town lay across the Thompson River, the desert behind the farm. The fruit trees produced and the garden flourished under irrigation - `Pop' claimed anything would grow on that land given water. In those days the land still provided for those that lived on it, but to supplement his income, Francis Morant also worked as a Provincial Game Warden. The stories he told of his travels on horseback and his encounters with wild animals, poachers and the natives enthralled young Morant. His father was held in great esteem in Nick's young and adventurous mind.

Neither of Nick's parents ever talked of their former lives in England, of grand-parents or the lifestyle they used to lead. But they did like to socialize with other immigrants of English background. In fact, often the social gatherings were polo, or cricket matches, a carryover from a former lifestyle. Recollections of the horses on the Morant farm prompt some of Nick's favorite stories of his boyhood:

We had quite a few horses over the years, never many at a time, never more than three. But I remember so well one horse named `Pongo' that I rode to school for several years. I went to a private tutor in North Kamloops, a little old lady; my people weren't too satisfied with the school system. I used to ride about a mile and a quarter every day.

Pongo was a grey. He had light colored eyes, almost pink. He was commonly known as an Indian Cayuse, and was next to human. He was an absolute character! People might find this hard to accept, that an animal has character, but believe me they do. Any dog owner would tell you that! Pongo was a name my father brought from South Africa, probably something very demeaning if you only knew it.

We used to hitch him to a two-wheeled pony cart. It was literally a pair of shafts and two wheels. You were seated at a point about five feet off the ground. With a good horse it was a fast means of transport, just as if you were jumping in your Volkswagen to go downtown to the supermarket. Pongo didn't care much for this rig. He would give lots of trouble being harnessed. He would deliberately back so that he was standing over the shafts and you couldn't raise them to put them in the slots over his shoulders. My Mom and Dad used to get furious with him when they were in a hurry and he'd act up. He'd look around at you when you got angry, with utter contempt in his eyes!

One of the things he would do, especially if you pushed him to go faster, was to stop dead, putting all four feet down. He would stand there, turn his head and look back at you around

Above: Kamloops was yet a frontier town in 1910 when Nick Morant was born. The Morant farm was just out of this photograph to the left, the bridge across the Thompson River led to downtown Kamloops. In the distance is the North Thompson and on its shore the Indian Reserve (white church), with Mt.Paul dominating the background. Morant made the photograph while quite young, circa 1928. *NMC*

Opposite page: Morant made this photograph along the placid South Thompson River just east of Kamloops at Campbell Creek. The mountain across the river is noted for a herd of Bighorn sheep that browse along its grassy slopes. The clay bluffs are lake benches that formed as a result of silt deposits from melting glaciers that filled a lake that stretched all the way down the Thompson River at the end of the last ice age. *NMC*

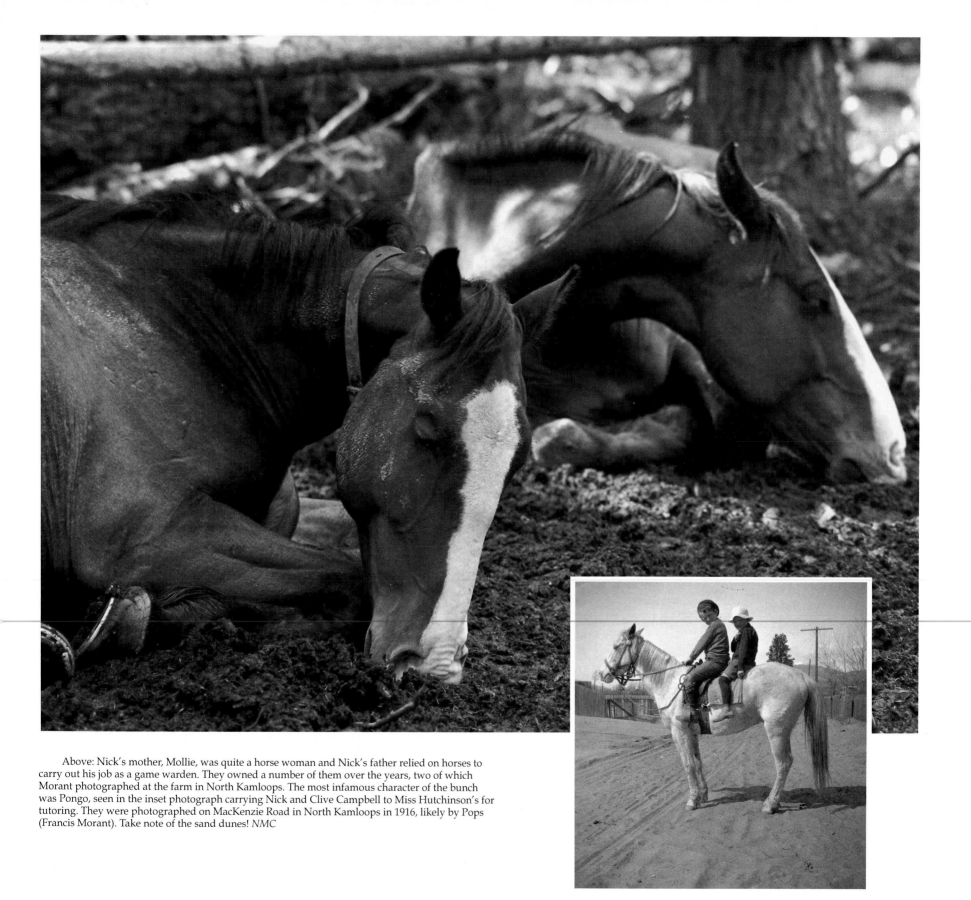

Above: Nick's mother, Mollie, was quite a horse woman and Nick's father relied on horses to carry out his job as a game warden. They owned a number of them over the years, two of which Morant photographed at the farm in North Kamloops. The most infamous character of the bunch was Pongo, seen in the inset photograph carrying Nick and Clive Campbell to Miss Hutchinson's for tutoring. They were photographed on MacKenzie Road in North Kamloops in 1916, likely by Pops (Francis Morant). Take note of the sand dunes! *NMC*

Pops at work on his stamp collection, circa 1928. *NMC*

In a photograph made by Willie circa 1944, Pops is trying out one of his "putt putt" boats that he was notorious for, while David, sitting, and Nick with the pole, occupy the dinghy, prepared to rescue it should Pops' vessel get away on him. *NMC*

Willie and Pops take a break from their hike up on the
hills above the Thompson River valley south of Kamloops.
Mt. Paul dominates the background behind them. The
country where Nick grew up lies in the rain shadow of the
Coast Mountains, and receives little precipitation.
Sagebrush, Ponderosa Pine and Bunchgrass prevail, cattle
ranching the only use for this arid land. *NMC*

the blinkers. My Mother had a number of expletives that she'd use that were lady-like ... sometimes. Then she'd give him another clip with the whip. That would be the last straw; he would promptly sit down on his backside in the dirt with his front legs splayed out; he'd just sit right back on the ground! If you were in town the villagers would laugh -you became the butt of the joke. That damned horse always won!

Recalling the the antics of Pongo would bring other stories to mind, particularly Nick's father's experiences with that horse:

One day Dad went over to the old brewery at the west end of Kamloops, the Rainier Brewing Company. He knew Mr.Lockie who was the chief engineer in charge of the steam engine that powered the plant. Lockie had promised Dad a barrel he needed. Promptly returning home with the new barrel, we found Pongo standing in the corral slumbering. Dad whispered to me, "let's play a trick on him!"

Our corral bordered on a sand hill with a ten degree slope leading down into the bottom where Pongo was standing. Dad got the new barrel out of the wagon, quietly opened the gate and let the barrel roll. Pongo took one look at it, waited till the barrel was about four feet from him, then let go with both hooves! I guarantee you there wasn't one single part of that barrel in one piece. When Dad returned to the brewery for another barrel, he had a lot of explaining to do to Mr.Lockie.

Another time, I went down to the stable to water another of one of our horses, and was surprised to see my Dad on Pongo, just sitting there outside the corral gate looking straight ahead. They were motionless and the horse had no bridle. It scared the hell out of me! I ran up and called out to Dad! "Get your Mother right away, hurry," he said.

He had been on his rounds as a game warden and had become snow blind. He was quite unable to see. Dad had turned Pongo around in the general direction of home and coaxed him forward. When they came to a fence, Pongo had enough sense to go to a gate and stop. Dad would get off, find the wire fence, let Pongo step in, go around, hold the reins, then close the gate. Finally he just took the bridle off entirely!

Pongo retraced his steps and brought Dad back to our gate where I found them that day.

Pongo got an extra feed of oats that night, redeemed at last!

One year of Nick's youth was spent attending an English boarding school when Mollie returned to her folks in England after a "falling out" between his parents:

She had had a slight difference of opinion with my father. She was very unhappy. If you read her poems, you could see a sadness in everything she wrote.

Mollie was a poetess of some note, and a friend of John Masefield, a very well known English poet.

Kamloops in those days was stark and barren, there were no trees. It was a desert. For anybody who had come out of an English home accustomed to cuckoos singing in the woods, then walked into this rough and ready place, it wasn't easy!

My Dad had a .38 revolver hung over the end of his bed all the years that we lived in that house because there wasn't much law and order. I think my Dad was a little worried about my Mom because she was a good looking woman. He was licensed to carry the gun because he was a warden, not that he took it uptown or wore it in public. But he was always alert. We also had a .22 pistol, and he used to take Mother down by the barn and shoot into the sand, just so she knew how to use it. I remember once, one of the cats was sick and dying. She said, "I'm not going to stand here and watch him dying this way." She got the pistol, I heard the `crack'! That was the end of the cat.

Coming from an English home as Mother did, the butler or the groom or somebody would have looked after the killing of the cat. It was a thing that is repugnant to an animal lover, yet you know you're doing the only humane thing.

Francis Morant, on the other hand, enjoyed the rough life, the wildness of the country and the lack of civilization. It was a man's life and he probably failed to see the

subservient existence a man's wife had in such a situation. So many English women who immigrated to the west with their men ended up being merely servants because there were no maids, unless they were extremely wealthy. What little money you had was needed, so you did the laundry yourself, and there were no washing machines! You washed the clothes by hand. To do them properly meant boiling them for a while, and in summertime that meant a hot kitchen. It might not have been as bad for Mollie as it was, perhaps, for the wives of the "sodbusters" on the prairies, but it remained a rigorous life.

This primitive life was something that the men enjoyed. It was a challenge for a young man to get out and go, get away from the social strata and regimentation of life in England. The young adventurer could find a certain degree of freedom non-existent back home. Nick sometimes saw his Mother crying and in those days could never understand why.

My education came out of a lot of the pleasures that my Mom and Dad should have enjoyed, but didn't. My Father did not believe in going to the show, and he would make it very difficult for my Mother if she wanted to go, by openly sulking and saying, "Oh well, if you want to spend the money, I suppose it's all right." He was cadging the odd penny because he had one thing in mind and that was that I should have a good education. They both suffered, giving up things they wanted for my welfare.

Francis Morant would make a thousand dollars a year out of the orchard, if he was lucky! His only other source of income was his job as a game warden. It was difficult looking after the orchard as he was often away on his rounds as warden, and one hundred and twenty five trees required considerable care. Today it would be tough to return even a thousand dollars because costs are so high, but their apples were in demand and commanded a reasonable price in a place where fresh produce was scarce.

Above: Pops entices the dog to do a trick for the camera, while Old Dickey stands steady, Mollie and David seated on his bare back. *NMC*

At right: Nick claimed Old Dickey was so gentle he would allow you to do anything on his back, and to prove it he had Willie make this picture of him sweeping the horses rump. Of course Old Dickey was probably more interested in the can of oats that Mollie had for him inside the barn window. *NMC*

My Mother used to go into town in a horse and buggy. She would put four boxes of apples in the wagon and as she went around town, if she saw somebody that she thought might buy some, usually someone she knew, she'd say, "You couldn't use a box of apples could you?" And I sometimes wonder if they just bought because they felt sorry for her.

She also, at one time, was delivering cordwood. In those days a cord of wood sold for six or eight dollars depending on what kind of wood it was. I remember that she ran afoul of a Kamloops socialite one day, a lady who treated her very badly because she was doing a man's work. Mother was somewhat of an oddity, even in those days. Women never indulged in a man's work! Some customers would get a man from the house to give her a hand; others would just sit there and disgustedly watch her do it.

Of course, Mother herself was from a good family, probably more deserving of status than this other woman who was well known as a socialite. Mother did a slow boil after the lady haughtily told her, "Tidy up my yard before you leave. I don't want any sticks lying around!" Mother was treated as lower than a parlour maid. She did a slow burn on this! One piece of wood after another was hurled down with increasing force, then the last one... she threw it right through the window!

This woman rushed to the window, "You're going to be charged for this!" My Mother said, "Don't worry, its paid for already, you'll get your load of wood for free." She came back and I remember Dad saying, "Jeese, we could have used the money, but maybe you were right!"

Formal schooling began for Nick when his father enrolled him in University Military School in Victoria. How the Morant's were able to afford such an education remains a mystery, for today that school, now known as University St. Michael's, is a very expensive proposition, and it was then, too. Attending that establishment proved to be a valuable experience for the young Morant, and though he failed in some areas to achieve scholastically, he was certainly well educated in the meaning of responsibility and common sense. Lasting friendships were formed, one of which would lead him to his career with Canadian Pacific; and certain talents were discerned which, when applied to that career, lent themselves to great success.

At the farm near Metchosin, on Vancouver Island, Willie had Nick and his mother, Mollie, lean on the corral fence together for a portrait. Intruding between them was Mollie's horse Trixie, demonstrating a decidedly contemptuous opinion of the subject at hand. *NMC*

I was enrolled in the University Military School in 1920 and left there in 1928 and was an absolute total flop as a student. All I could manage was 13% in my McGill entrance exams! The only thing I did well in was English Composition and French.

Dad knew I tried; the Masters were unanimous in that belief. I was a Prefect in charge of discipline in one of the school dormitories and I think that's where I might have got misled. When you're a Prefect you are on your own; you are considered pretty much an adult in the school colony. You're not on a first name basis with the Masters, but next thing to it because if there's anything wrong in the school, and its in your dormitory, you have to answer to them.

I was happy as hell there - it all suited me fine. I came home twice a year. I stayed at the school for roughly two halves. I didn't take any of the short holidays like Easter or Thanksgiving. I was quite happy to do that because the fare, which was nothing by today's standards, would be saved, and my tuition there was about $2,000.00 a year!

I once had an invitation to spend my summer holiday with a boy from Japan. I didn't realize it then, but this idea would have been a heart-breaker for my Mother, who looked forward so much to having me home. But at age 16 I wanted to go. I thought it was a great idea. Kids are totally selfish; they're too young not to be. Later on they develop responsibility.

I had quite decided to accept. Dad told me that if I really wanted to go he would find the

Who is the "ham" here, Morant or the horse? *NMC*

money, but that he didn't 'have too much going' just then. After I thought about it and realized the money problem, I changed my mind. As circumstances would have it, I luckily stayed home, avoiding the danger my friend became involved in when an earthquake hit Japan.

He had just boarded a Canadian Pacific ship in Yokohama to return when the earthquake occurred. The wharf tilted, causing a shipment of power poles that had been stacked on the dock to roll down on the people waving goodbye, right in front of his eyes. The Empress of Asia remained there for four days helping the injured.

Winnipeg winters are harsh, as attests this photograph Morant made while in the employ of the <u>Winnipeg Free Press</u> in 1935. However there is a certain beauty in this photograph that reminds many of times past, or tells the younger generations what life used to be like. *NMC*

CHAPTER TWO
Quest For A Career

*L*et's go from what I would like to call the happy days when I was in Victoria, to the times that followed immediately after I left University School.

I went through the usual period of hiatus when you don't know what the hell you can do because you have no experience. Wherever you go somebody says, "Have you ever done this sort of thing before?" You say, "No."

I had an idea that I'd like to be a newspaper reporter, a writer. My parents were helpful. Whatever I wanted to do was fine with them. But with an 18 year-old boy on their hands, and they're stuck in Kamloops, British Columbia, which in those days was somewhat of an unheard of spot, how were they to help me? It was 1928, a time when the depression was already in progress and things were not very good.

Where do you turn if you're a farmer in Kamloops, to find help in a case like this? It was a question of knowing an editor or a publisher.

Mollie tried - she had friends who were on the Manchester Guardian back in England. Who though, would want to take on a kid with no experience. As Nick recalled:

The very first job I managed to get, was somewhat unrelated, but I suppose directly aligned with newspaper work. I got a job with an old gentleman who came from Dryden, Ontario. The man's name was De Hurst. He was a very distinguished gent in his 70's, always smartly dressed. He wore a light colored riding habit, high boots and a white shirt, which was always spotless. In fact he looked like Cecil B.DeMille on a Ten Commandments set.

Mr.De Hurst, of Dutch origin, arrived in North Kamloops with a dream. This was to take advantage of the hidden wealth to be harvested from the thousands of Ponderosa Pine trees in the dry belt areas of B.C. He contracted with the chiefs of the local Siwash Indian tribes to gather

pine cones in gunnysacks. Simply put - the cones were placed in drying racks in an upper room that was heated to a stifling 90 degrees Fahrenheit. My job was to load the cones on these racks and when the cones expanded they were dumped into a big revolving cylinder that would separate the seeds from the pinecones. In addition I learned to service the electric motors, saw they were properly oiled and the belts were in good shape. That was all there was to it, but it was the heat that made it a difficult assignment. It made me realize right away that if I couldn't do something with my head somewhere along the way, this was to be the way I'd spend the rest of my life - doing a dirty job for somebody else. Mind you, as a kid I was glad to have that job and Mr. De Hurst was always nice, kind and thoughtful. He realized how hot it was up there!

I got 14 bucks a week, and my parents were adamant that I pay rent, if for no other reason than to make me realize what happens when you get your pay cheque. You suddenly find that most of it goes to food and lodging, so you've got nothing left to go to the show or take your gal out.

In the interim, Nick's mother had a letter from friends on the <u>Manchester Guardian</u> who were honest enough to discourage her, saying that, as in North America, experienced reporters everywhere were out of work. However, an opportunity did arise, through the school Nick had just left, to meet an editor of the <u>Victoria Colonist,</u>who said he would be glad to meet him and help in any way he could.

During the interview, the feeling that I had was that I was being given the runaround by a person who should have been more honest about the employment situation but who was afraid to state the real truth. This man's lack of courage created a resolve in me never to act in this manner - but always to face the real situation no matter how unpleasant.

I had gone to Victoria at my parent's expense, where it was agreed that I should go for a walk with him on Sunday morning. I fell in step as we started our stroll around the esplanade of Beacon Hill Park. He talked about the responsibilities of the newspapers to the public - a lot of 'high-falutin' ideals - absolutely nothing tangible. But he failed to say, "Would I like a job as an office boy in the newsroom?"

It is no use thinking that anyone can hire on as a reporter just like that. He refused to say, "Look kid, there's hundreds of experienced newspaper writers and reporters and editors fanning their asses on the street, selling apples because there is no work for them. So don't expect an early start in your case." He let on that there was a great future for a young fellow in the press.

He gave me to understand very clearly what I should do when I got back to Kamloops... "If you see a good story let us have it, we'd like to use it - we'll pay you for it." That's as far as it ever went.

I returned to Kamloops. I wasn't happy with what had happened - disappointed would be putting it lightly. The next thing I knew, I heard there was a crossing accident on the CNR. I hopped on my bicycle and rode seven miles, taking a piece of note paper with me. I found some wreckage, though everything had been tidied up, cars gone, nothing worth a photograph. I got the victims' names from the police, wrote up a story and wired it collect to the news desk. Of course they had already received the story from Canadian Press, but nobody ever mentioned Canadian Press to me, I'd never heard anything about them.

I soon received a very curt letter from the editor asking by what authority I had filed this story, hooking them for a non-press rate on the wire. But they were the ones at fault. The editor had encouraged me with false ideas that, as it happened, kicked back on everybody concerned. They had to pay for a wire at excessive rates on an un-newsworthy story. I was frustrated and upset since I thought I had my first story.

Because of that incident during my youth, today, when anyone comes to me and asks me how they might get a job like mine, I am very hard on them. It is no use giving a kid a false story. If things were tough for me, well, they're going to be just as tough for them and they might as well know now rather than be disappointed and led into believing certain things because some well-meaning guy has fed them a line. You can see why sometimes I'm accused of being destructive or pessimistic in my approach to young people, but they have to face reality sooner or later!

Many times I have told young people just that! How many guys in Canada have got a job such as mine - freedom to go anywhere, do practically what I want when I want? There are just bloody few jobs like that! So if you think that mine is that great, you're right, but let me tell you, there aren't many around for the picking!

Most jobs, that of a newspaper photographer, for instance, are harassing, endless and thankless. There's no particular joy in doing the routine dull things that happen on most newspapers - at least this is my view. For every murder, for every interesting story, there are twenty that involve the 'Amalgamated Women of North America' holding their annual meeting in some back room of the local ELKs Hall. But I always remember this as one of the vital stepping-stones that I had to get across without blowing my frustrated brains out - but it wasn't easy!

Bang! The window shutter struck the side of the house as the wind picked up and moaned through the lodge-pole pines. The high-pitched cry of a coyote carried in the wind, answered seconds later by the yipping of another. In the living room of the cozy Morant home in Banff, we listened to the sounds of nature as the fire flickered in the glowing embers. We sat silently, eager for our host to continue:

I suppose I'd worked for about a year in the cone factory. I didn't have too much money, and I was getting in my parents' hair. One day, I got on my bike and rode down to the CPR station. This was a big thing to do in small towns in those days. People would go down in their cars and park. The train would roll in, people would be waiting on the platform to get on, others would get off. The mail would be unloaded and up front the engines would be exchanged. You often recognized people, or friends, and could get the latest gossip about who was going where or doing what. The simple pleasures of country folk in the early thirties!

I arrived that day and was sitting on my bike, one foot on the pedal, my curiosity aroused by a different railway coach near the front of the train that looked like an observation car. Not knowing too much about private cars or what's known as business cars, I didn't realize what it was. I just thought it was an observation car they had up front for some reason.

A young man got off whose face looked familiar, and who was it but my old school chum Jimmy Coleman. He was then just a year or so behind me still attending University School. His Dad was Vice-President of Western Lines for the CPR in Winnipeg. Jimmy was riding home on his father's private car.

While traveling on his father's car one of Jimmy's pet games was to secrete a .22 caliber pistol in his baggage and shoot at insulators as he went along the line. Employees on the railway would wonder how in the hell there was a whole bunch of these things cracked off! Little did they know this damage originated from one of the Vice-Presidential business cars.

All through University School Jimmy and I used to pull off the worst pranks, but we had fun! He was in my dormitory at University School for four years. As a Prefect there for six years I was always in charge of the junior house.

I had 60 kids before I left and I was completely responsible for them - where they went, what they did, or for that matter, what they didn't do. Everything! Anybody got in trouble ... too much noise or fighting ... the Masters came to see me. It was marvellous training in handling people.

Anyway, Jimmy got off... "Haven't seen you in a long time. What are you doing?" he asked.

"Not much of anything, just working in a cone factory," I replied, "but I'm job hunting!"

"What are you trying to get into?" he responded. I told him how I hoped I might get into reporting on a newspaper somewhere.

"It must be pretty tough getting anything in this place," he said.

"Yes", I said, "that's true. The local newspaper is not very big and besides with three experienced reporters they've got more than enough staff for this small town, so they're not likely to want an 18 year-old whom they're going to have to train."

In response Jimmy said, "Did you know there is a Public Relations department in the CPR that employs writers? Dad isn't with me, he came out, but went back through the States, but I'm going to ask him about it when I get back to Winnipeg."

Jimmy himself pursued a writing career, was a very well read sports columnist for many years, and ended up in the Sports Writers Hall of Fame. His interests and mine were never all that far apart. I never did get a letter back from Jimmy, who even at that age was too busy playing the racing sheet to write.

I had virtually written off any possibilities with the CPR when I received a telegram signed by D.C.Coleman, Vice-President of Western Lines, Canadian Pacific Railway. It said; "If it is convenient to you, would you kindly report to Mr.J.E.March, Press Representative, Canadian Pacific Railway, in Winnipeg. You can have an interview with him..." and so forth. I have since been forever grateful to Jimmy for his recommendation.

I rather thought that I had the job `in the bag' even though the letter just offered an interview. What clothes should I take? What should I do with the motorcycle? Important things like that!

On the appointed day, January 18, 1929, a young Nicholas Morant went to the CPR offices in Winnipeg and was introduced to a delightful man for whom he was to work for the next 25 years. His name was Edgar March and he later transferred to Montreal as the guru of the PR Department where he dealt with internal and external problems in the organization. He was a well known figure in the corridors of Windsor Station - the head offices of Canadian Pacific.

A very popular man, March would sit talking for hours on the telephone with no apparent heed to business at hand. He was a walking encyclopedia when it came to someone seeking information as to whom to see about a new rug or which person in the vice president's office handled pass applications. Nick speaks retrospectively of his first interview with March...

Of course, I was shaking in my boots when I went to see him, even though my job was assured by Mr.Coleman's interest. People in the outside office knew there was a new guy coming, all eyes were on me and I felt awkward, nervous and embarrassed and I guess I behaved that way. Mr.March had a talk with me and told me that I was hired. I couldn't have known it, but everyone there knew it was a forgone conclusion They wouldn't have had me come down if that hadn't been the case. The reason that I had been invited was solely because I was a classmate of the Vice-President's son, and how important those things are when you're looking for a job. In other words, the old school tie saved the day.

I well remember going down to Winnipeg. I got the ticket and it was understood that I would have two days' hotel paid, whether I joined the company or not. I set out in the world and stayed at the Royal Alexandra Hotel. It was 'the' hotel in Winnipeg in those days. The only thing was that I found out breakfast was a buck and a quarter in the main dining room and that strained my reserves; they were about to be strained a hell of a lot more!

The starting wage was $90 a month; benefits included a limited railway pass...

At one time in my career I had an all-lines annual CP pass, an all lines annual Canadian National pass, a telegraph frank with which I could send a wire anywhere in the country, and an express pass. I could ship any number of times to anywhere in Canada. It was very handy when I lived in hotels before moving into the house in Banff, but with the government takeover of passenger services, I lost them. I don't have any passes at all now! And now there is no passenger train!

A shepherd and his dog herd sheep in the dry
Ponderosa Pine country above Kamloops, B.C., circa 1935.
NMC

Portfolio I

The Prairies and The West

The Qu'Appelle Valley, Saskatchewan. *NMC*

Prairie elevators, Airdrie, Alberta. *NMC*

Harvest on the prairies, an old time threshing machine, location unknown. *NMC*

Prairie elevators, location unknown. *NMC*

Above: The sugar beet harvest, Raymond, Alberta. *NMC*

Previous page: A parade of brand new Massey-
Ferguson combines harvest grain east of Calgary, Alberta.
NMC

A Case combine works the fields in the foothills west of Olds, Alberta. The distinctive peak in the Front Range of the Rockies, above the windmill, is the Devils Head (9890'), and is located near the headwaters of the Ghost River. *NMC*

Morant made this photograph of downtown Calgary
from the roof of Canadian Pacific's Palliser Hotel in 1937.
The hotel is named in honour of Captain John Palliser who
commanded an expedition (1857-1860) to determine the
economic prospects of the Canadian west along the 49th
Parallel and the feasibility of a railway route along the
border. *NMC*

The world famous Calgary Stampede chuckwagon races were captured by Morant in 1937, Dick Cosgrave's outfit in the lead. Cosgrave won 10 championships, the only competitor to have done so, and retired to become arena director for the Stampede from 1943 on. *NMC*

Relaxation after a hard day on the range. *NMC*

Settling down for a night on the range. *NMC*

The Professor and his dogs, Winnipeg, Manitoba, circa 1936. *NMC*

CHAPTER THREE
Moonlighting On The CPR

Feet on his desk, tie askew, Edgar March explained Nick's new position with the CPR. "I won't tell you what you've got to do," he said. "Your duties will be varied, perhaps a little bit of a glorified office boy at times and," he paused, "others will find some things for you to do and certainly you will have to take your turn at clipping newspapers." Nick explains:

What happened when you did newspaper clippings was, you cut an article from a newspaper: "Honorable J.J.Manion Says Railways In Bad Shape." The body of the clipping went on: "Fort William...." You take the complete clipping, write a short note on its contents, and file it under an appropriate heading. Two weeks or a month later, somebody would come in from one of the offices and ask, "Was there a clipping in the Fort William Times Journal on a Thursday, one, two or three weeks ago having to do with the plight of the railroads?"

You reply, "Yes, I think it was in the Monday's paper two weeks ago!" As you talk you look up the thing quite quickly. You go right to the copy of the paper in your files and there it is!

Not only do you clip papers, but you memorize everything that passes before your eyes, and in many cases you're using your own judgement to determine what the company officers need. For instance, if you see a story there of the Brandon City Council replying to complaints of excessive noise from the railway, perhaps crossing bells keeping people awake at night. That is clipped and sent up to the Vice-President's office from where it is forwarded to the Superintendent's office in Brandon.

It was an interesting position to be in, right in the midst of the company's affairs. Morant clipped every weekly and daily newspaper in Canada for at least three or four years. Every little town had a paper,

and each article pertaining to the CPR was noted and filed. It only followed that the company maintained a close rapport with the newspapers, utilizing them for public relations and advertising purposes across Canada.

Getting back to the interview with Mr.March; Nick related that March graciously offered the use of a room in the CPR hotel for a month until he could find a place to live...

But what he didn't tell me was that you didn't get paid any money from the CPR for the first 30 days! They provided the room, but not any food.

I had a rough time of it! I didn't want to ask my folks for any more money, so I used to walk miles to a cheap boarding house; it was a dreadful place, but what an education it was to see how other people lived. It was something to discover what a miserable existence some people had to endure.

Just as I was leaving Mr.March's office he said, "By the way, Nick, when you go home - we quit at five - will you do me a small favor?"

"Certainly, sir," I replied.

"Just drop in and if I'm asleep, wake me," he said.

Time and time again I'd go in and wake him; "Mr.March, time to go -it's five o'clock!"

"Oh yes. Thanks, Nick. Goodnight!"

He'd go get his hat and follow down the corridor behind me. Jolly man!

It was a happy place to work. I remember one girl that worked in the office with us. I still phone Myrtle Lewis long distance in Winnipeg today, and we talk about those times. A group of us used to go skinny-dipping in the quarries north of town. Eight or ten people with not a shred of clothing on!

Shortly after Morant started with the CPR in 1929, he met "Willie," nineteen-year-

old Ivy Young, a telephone operator at the Winnipeg Grain Exchange. "Willie" was Ivy's nickname, a name used as a coverup during phone calls taken or made by Nick from CPR offices.

Ivy was born in Fort William, Ontario, in 1910 and had three brothers. Her family was not well off, consistently battling financial problems and unemployment. They never enjoyed a permanent home and were continually on the move as circumstances overtook them. Their survival as a family depended on every penny the children could earn, but amazingly they all became very successful in their careers and were outstanding people.

Ivy had a very good friend in Winnipeg in Norah Helliwell. Ivy and Norah got into a lot of mischief, but managed to stay out of any serious trouble, relying on each other for support.

One day, shortly after Nick had hired on with the CPR, there was a spectacular fire on Lombard Street, near the Grain Exchange. Nick went down to watch the commotion and made some photographs of it. Amongst the spectators were Norah and Ivy. They saw Morant making the pictures and asked if he were a newspaper man. Making their introductions, they left and went to Child's Restaurant for coffee, where they pursued their acquaintance. From that night on the fire was lit between Ivy and Nick!

They rarely went a day without seeing each other from then on, but it was several years before they considered marriage. During the depression era, jobs were at a premium, and there was no recourse but to delay marriage for the time being. Ivy's family needed her financial help. A woman who married would be obligated to give up her job, and Nick made little money as it was. So they dined together and spent what time they could with each other between working hours. A job was a very precious thing in those days, and Nick took great satisfaction in working for the CPR, finally having found his niche in life.

The people Nick worked with were wonderful, and the job was flexible enough that if you did it well, no one kept track of you or watched over your shoulder. Nick was often alone in the office at lunchtime...

Permit me to make some observations from a young office boy quickly acclimatizing himself to the rigors of the world in 1930. If you stayed on and covered the office at lunch break the regular crew would lose track of you completely. As soon as the first man was back from lunch - you disappeared. It was good for an extra fifteen minutes anytime. As one grew more expert and flushed with your own success you would eventually reappear carrying a file that you parked with a fellow office boy nearby.

The PR office was really a family affair - our mentors were our bosses. Of course ... people like Edgar March and Hughie Campbell - who advised me what to do in case of an emergency... "Admit Nothing!" *On inter-office correspondence...* "Always answer the letter even if it is written like a child's essay - make it so simple they can't grasp the situation."

"It was a very happy madhouse really. One day we were all expecting Travers Coleman (a cousin of Jimmy Coleman) to arrive to take over a new job. The doors in offices in those days were often made of a translucent `frosted glass.' One could see a figure at the door but it was a ghostly image really - nothing could be seen in recognizable detail. That morning the door was kicked rather roughly and we could easily distinguish a stout figure wearing a bowler hat. Work stopped. Slowly the door opened - maybe six inches... then a hand reached in, grasping the inside doorknob. The door jerked a bit wider. As soon as the opening was wide enough a heavily built figure appeared. A round face was now evident -it was a guileless moon face... full moon. The visitor's eyes were suddenly opened very wide and the eyes rolled around in the skull. At the same moment, Coleman leaned his bowler back against the door frame, causing the

Willie enjoying the view of the Rideau Canal out her hotel window in Ottawa, 1948. The parliament buildings are in the background. *NMC*

hat to lift in a full 45 degree turn. The effect was that of a clown in the country circus.

He stepped forward a pace and introduced himself. "I'm Coleman." His hat was back in a normal position for the first time since he had arrived. Mr.Coleman was a much loved figure - his name is still remembered up and down the Pacific Coast - on both sides of the border. Not so much for his prowess in PR, rather more for his maniacal imitation of a wrestling match, wherein he is both of the central figures as well as the referee.

There was yet another celebrated person who could be as outlandish as the devil when encouraged. Miss Bessie James, onetime PR for the CPR in Chicago. One day I was working on clippings when she reached across her desk for the phone. She stopped, and looked up at me slyly. "Nicholas," she said, "you aren't looking

at my bosom are you?"

She happened to be very well endowed. I didn't know which way to look and before I could think of a better answer, I replied,

"Yes I was." It was the truth, I had been!

So the clippings were clipped, stacked on a piece of paper with the dateline and name of the newspaper, and then they were sorted and sent to various senior officials of the company so that they knew what was going on in their area. Along with that job, I did a little bit of writing as well, producing releases for the newspapers regarding company affairs in communities along the line. At that period (about 1932) in my Public Relations career I began to discover that the CPR was not able to get the photographs they needed for modern press coverage. At this juncture we have one of the minor turning points of my career.

We were using hired photographers to make pictures of various celebrated people that might be arriving in Winnipeg. When we tipped the newspapers of an arriving personage, they would blankly inquire, "Lord Watingbottom, what does he do?"

And we'd say, "Well, he's the comptroller of Farbin," or some such company as that.

Not being front page material, the newspaper people would say, "I guess we might do something, but we can't very well send our man down." So we would hire a photographer.

We had a still photographer under contract to us, Mr.L.B.Foote of the firm Foote and James on Main Street. Mr.James was a very cautious gentleman; he did the portraiture. Mr.Foote did all the outside work, with an 8x10 camera; buildings, construction, etc. Foote was a tall skinny fellow. He was quite a character; and was on a first name basis with all the young people in the Royal Family, because anytime any members visited Winnipeg, they came by train. It was the only way to travel!

Foote would always be down there with his 8X10 camera and a device on the front of the lens that was known as a Thornton-Picard shutter. You pulled a red tassle and then you released the shutter with an air release exactly as you might use today, and the exposure was perhaps a fifth or half second.

He would say, "Now that's it, now then, steady there." Bump-tin-too! "That's wonderful."

And he'd make another one, huge glass plates that had to be handled carefully. It took quite a while.

One year I was present, matter of fact, when the Duke of Windsor came out.

"By gawd," the Duke said, "look here, first person we see is old Foote, and I thought he was dead long ago!"

He remembered Foote from all the thousands of photographers that must have confronted him. Mind you, Foote was a delightful fellow, great sense of humor, and rank didn't impress him - he'd talk to anybody!

But Mr.Foote was not making the kind of pictures the newspaper photographers of the era were doing. He wasn't making pictures with

flash, except with his powder, and so he found himself in exactly the same state then as I am now. I could see that there was an opening here for somebody who took pictures the way the press were taking them and not the way commercial photographers did.

So I began to make photographs for the Company. I was greatly encouraged by the people I worked with; Bessie James, who was the Women's Press Representative, and Mr.Hugh Campbell, who took over March's job when he transferred to Montreal.

On the bank of the Kicking Horse River, just west of Field, B.C., at a railway siding named Emerald, Morant made this photograph of Willie amidst the beautiful landscape of the Rockies. The peaks to the north are up the Amiskwi (from the Cree indian word meaning "beaver tail") River Valley. *NMC*

Campbell was as much a character as March had been. He was a real down to earth guy. He just loved it when I once sarcastically said, "Look, maybe we could make a better picture of this if we put a cowboy in it. A cowboy on his horse..., give it a little glamour."

Campbell looked at me and said, "You know the definition of a cowboy? (He was from Ft.MacLeod, Alberta)... F_____g farmhand on a horse!"

How true. He was a hard nut, but human. He taught me an awful lot about meeting and handling people.

Campbell once worked for the Calgary Herald as a reporter when the infamous Bob Edwards was in his heyday. (Edwards was the colorful proprietor of the Calgary Eyeopener newspaper). Edwards was once giving a political speech in Edmonton that Campbell was assigned to cover. He met Edwards coming into the hall and asked if he had an `advance' of his speech. In other words, the speaker would carry a half dozen or so copies of his speech and any member of the press who wanted a copy to take back to the office could get one for background reference when writing the story.

Everything was fine. Edwards smiled, "Ah yes my boy, glad to have you with us. Here's a copy of my speech."

So Campbell wrote a story and the next day when he went back to Calgary, he caught hell. "What are you writing about?" asked his editor.

"I had an advance copy of the speech from Edwards and I reported on that," Campbell said.

What had happened was that Edwards was a little drunk that evening and he had given Campbell his original speech, the only copy he had! So now, slightly under the influence, he had to extemporize. He shot the speech off the cuff as best he could, but a lot of things were totally changed. Poor Hughie was caught in the middle.

Campbell said he should have known that this was Edwards' own copy, but he didn't recognize it until he started to read it. There would be a typed line that would say, "And moreover, if elected we are going to see that those things are done!"

And then in Edwards' own handwriting against the margin, "At this point pause for cries from the gallery of `good ole Bob.'"

Getting back to the subject, that was how I started doing photography quite seriously. I could see that old Foote wasn't able to fill the bill for the Public Relations Department. I still had to do clippings, I still had to write stories about Mediterranean cruises, but what I really enjoyed was getting out of the damned office. I didn't mind coming in at night and working for two hours getting the clippings up to date; as long as I did that my job was assured.

Bessie James and my boss, Hugh Campbell, started doing all kinds of things to cover up for me as I started to drift about town as a self-styled photojournalist. They created accounts and bought things, ostensibly for office stores, some of which happened to be chemicals for developing, or some such other thing. They did it only because it was to their advantage to get the pictures they wanted in the papers and they found I could make them.

Everyone began covering for me. I had a tacit agreement, quite unspoken, with Mr.Campbell. He didn't care what the dickens I did as long as my primary job was done! If I were out of the CPR offices taking pictures for the newspapers and there was a disturbance down the street, everyone who worked at the station joked that Nick Morant, the CPR public relations man, was now taking part in a riot. Nobody said anything about my sideline. They all knew what I was doing. They were all very kind, including senior officers who were secretly on my side. For instance, Mr.Coleman, who was Vice-President at that time in Winnipeg, used to be a newspaperman himself. Jimmy Coleman, his son, my former classmate, became a very famous Canadian sportswriter! All these people were on my side, though they didn't officially know a thing about it.

As a matter of course I began freelancing - moonlighting if you will! I changed my domicile to a small downtown hotel, the St.Regis, to be closer to the newspaper offices. I was a hundred yards from the Winnipeg Tribune, five hundred yards from the Free Press. So, if I had a picture that I thought might sell, I would beat it over to one or the other. If I didn't sell to the Tribune, I had only to go another five hundred yards to try the Free Press.

Towards the end it got to the point where the Free Press city editors would say, "Did you cover that thing last night for the Tribune?"

And I'd say, "Yes."

And they said, "Don't take them everything, give us a break!."

So it finally got to the point where I could bring anything to the Free Press and be pretty sure of selling it because they would rather have me taking pictures for them than getting scooped by the Tribune. I certainly realized the advantage of this, but made it a habit not to `kill the goose that laid the golden egg.'

During those hectic times I was able to make one or two quite startling pictures. One was of a pedestrian being knocked over by a police motorcycle during a riot, and later another of the Winnipeg fire chief running for his life as a brick wall was collapsing on him. All this was done on the Company's time. I would nip out of the office, Campbell and Bessie minding the shop. They even fixed me up with a crude darkroom. True it was a filthy hole next to a chimney where an old public toilet used to be, but it served my purpose. I had to plug all the openings in the wall to prevent light seeping in, but it had running water by the sink and that was the big thing.

When I moved to the St.Regis Hotel, I established a darkroom there. The hotel, though a second class establishment, was clean, and located in the centre of the city. Interestingly enough two of the managers there ended up as managers of the Banff Springs Hotel in later years. I used to develop pictures under the shoe-black stand. Guys were sitting up on the high stool and I crouched down inside with the door blocked and that's where I developed my film. Then, I had an enlarging machine that was homemade. I used the camera that I took the pictures with, a 6 1/2x8 1/2 Ross Reflex view camera, and I made enlargements in the bedroom, then ran down and washed them in the men's room next to the beer parlour.

The result was, as you can well imagine, some guys would stagger in; "Hey, look at this guy, look at these pictures here in the wastebasket!"

"What's this all about?"

"What're you doing these here for?"

"Well," I'd say, "this is the only place I've

got."

It was awfully hard when I went into the newspaper offices and I'd see their darkrooms all fixed up with real enlargers, and I'm having to compete against these guys with nothing.

Compete I did, though, and I was able to get the scoop on a lot of things because I had my own secret service -tipsters! Veteran's Cab would phone me up in the middle of the night and say;

"There's a pretty good fire up in the north end, you wanna go up?"

I would say, "Sure."

In exchange for the fare and the tip I might make a good photograph, but more than often the cost of the trip would exceed what I would get paid for the photos. When the picture was published though, I would have the byline, and recognition as the photographer was the important thing; you had to establish your name.

I had two ladies of the street who lived in a house across from the hotel and I had them working for me too. They would ring me in the middle of the night and say they'd seen something. Sometimes they were good tips; sometimes they were phony ones, or by the time I got there whatever was happening was over and the taxi fare wasted. Those two women were very interesting, though. They were both old enough to be my mother, but I used to go and sit in their kitchen and talk over a cup of tea. There would, of course, be the odd interruption! Strange gentlemen would appear in the background and vanish upstairs, then one of the ladies would excuse herself. While I continued chatting with the other, the first would reappear and make herself a cup of tea. They never once propositioned me. Ordinary everyday people, sitting around talking about the state of the nation!

I also had fellows that worked with the street railway. In those days they used to employ inspectors who stood out in all kinds of weather at key points, with notebooks, keeping track of the streetcars. They had phone boxes along the street from which they could relay any problems to their superiors, or inform me of anything that

was happening. These men would be out in -40F degree weather, just standing around waiting for streetcars to go by at 2am - an awful job! Mr.Cousins, a great pal and very a useful spy, often alerted me to all manner of things because when accidents happened around town, the streetcar system was often affected or involved. The fact that the street railway didn't like publicity regarding accidents didn't curb my contact, as Mr.Cousins trusted me implicitly and knew I wouldn't divulge my sources

So I became established as a news photographer, you might say - a freelancer. The CPR Public Relations Department was still my employer. The Free Press was buying nearly everything I gave them. The times were eventful; this was the depression era and the period of unrest that led up to the infamous Winnipeg riots. People were getting hurt; a man was killed not fifty feet away from me, but it happened on the other side of a billboard and I didn't see it. The Tribune photographer Claude Dettloff got the shot. He had an uncanny ability to be where something was happening.

Just before the incident he said to me; "Well, I'm going to go around the corner and see what's going on; there's nothing too healthy here!"

So he went around the billboard and here were two guys beating a policeman to death. They had uprooted a fence post to do him in. Then we were all in trouble because they called the Tribune photographer as a witness to the picture he made, which certainly didn't help the two guys who were on their way to the hangman.

What was interesting in all this was how the CPR continued to back me. Then the big day came when I was offered a job with the Free Press. So now I was torn between my loyalty to the Company, to the people who had been supporting me all this time. It was a question of whether it was fair to leave.

One evening I waited till the staff had all gone home and went to talk to Mr.Campbell. I remember we both stood looking out the window when I told him; "I've been offered a job with the Free Press, they're going to pay me $35.00 a week," which was more than I made at the CPR.

I said to him, "Do you think I should take it?"

Now he could have said, "If I were you, I would stay here."

He could have said that and I'd have been inclined to stay, but he was big enough that he replied, "This is your big chance. What I'd do if I were you - go to the Free Press. Sure, we'll miss you here, but you'll probably find that you'll get right back again with the company if you want, perhaps in a better situation. Put in say two or three years with the Free Press and you'll be able to come back with tremendous experience."

I left the CPR and went to the Free Press. CPR staff gave me a cuckoo clock as a parting gift, which said something about these people since it cost at least six bucks, a great deal of money in the thirties. Everybody agreed the cuckoo clock went to the right guy. Then four years later I was back again - with the cuckoo. I didn't last all that long with the Free Press, perhaps fortunately, as I'd probably still have been there. The chief photographer, in the end when he left, had a $40 a month pension!

The plowman and his team. Manitoba, 1935. *NMC*

Nicholas Morant

68

CHAPTER FOUR
On The Free Press - 1935

*N*ow I was on the Free Press - a real newspaper photographer at last! I had been hired by the publisher to; "brighten up my newspaper." Anybody who has been around will recognize my situation in as much as fellow photo staffers were concerned. Harry Steel, whom I knew well from my earlier freelancing days was not as friendly as he used to be. He was senior photographer but I was the fair-haired boy menacing his future. For some time Harry was cool toward me, but he became more mellow as the days wore on. In time I realized he was having trouble with focusing and I learned that he was in fact, suffering from the effects of cataracts, an affliction that I myself now suffer. Steel and I were to become lifetime friends.

The days on the Free Press were not always the exciting reporter's forays that the movies usually show. Generally nothing exciting happened around Winnipeg. On a typical day, as Morant describes;

You'd go into the editorial room and receive your assignments. You'd be assigned, as I once was, to make a picture of a guy who was going to demonstrate a non-exploding gas tank. The Fire Chief and a lot of city hall people were to be there. Boil gasoline in a gas tank! Crazy!

I went down to see the demonstration and made some pictures of this fellow boiling the gas..., nothing happened! No explosion!

What it proved I don't know, but when I came back in the next morning, the editor asked, "Got your pictures of the gas tank?"

I said, "Have 'em right here."

I handed them to him. "Son of a gun," he said, "it didn't blow up!"

That was the end of that story - into the trash can!

The Free Press editorial room, city desk, 1936. At the main desk, left to right, is Orton Grain, unknown, Frank Wilson and Ted Dafoe. The center figure is Frank Morris (who became well known as a Toronto drama critic) and at the far right is Mr.Hand, the city editor, likely reading the Tribune. In the close foreground is Ted Boothe, the Free Press message runner. *NMC*

Sometimes there are events that happen in an individual's life that are turning points - things happen that can alter one's entire life depending on which route you take. William Shakespeare very aptly wrote in Julius Caesar:

There is a tide in the affairs of men,
Which, taken at the flood, leads on to
  fortune;
Omitted, all the voyage of their life
Is bound in shallows and in miseries.
On such a full sea are we now afloat,
And we must take the current when it
  serves,
Or lose our ventures.

One day after I'd been with the Free Press about three years, I was sent to Brandon to make some pictures of an agricultural meeting. It was typical of newspaper photography: there was always an endless array of mundane affairs to cover.

On the way back I made a photograph of a man plowing a field with his team of horses. It was a beautiful spring day. Since the Free Press is largely oriented to the agricultural scene, I thought that the photograph was newsworthy and could be of some use to the paper.

I put this in with the pictures of the farmers' meeting and turned the material over to the news editor, the senior editor of the daily paper, Mr.Abbey Coo. Abbey was a guy who was not exactly the artist's friend. He was president of the Canadian Amateur Hockey Association, if I remember correctly, and was a little bit more talented with pucks than he was with a paint

69

brush.

Anyway, when I showed him the pictures, he glanced through them the way he usually did with no good words and maybe no bad words, but if there were any words at all, the first ones would be bad.

When he came to the picture of the plowman he said,

"What the hell is this?"

"Who asked for a photograph like this?"

"Nobody," I replied, "I just made it on the way."

"Well, if nobody asked you to make it, why bother me with it?" He threw it away!

I was just a little bit upset, but thought to myself, "Oh well, I should have known better!"

So, crestfallen, I retrieved the picture from the wastebasket.

In those days the typical editorial rooms were great expanses of row upon row of desks, some with people madly typing away, others sitting around smoking and discussing some pressing issue. It was just as you might see in one of the old movies like "The Front Page," an incredible hive of people and noise.

As I walked back across the editorial room, a man bumped into me. It was T.B.Roberton, the associate editor of the newspaper and assistant to J.W.Dafoe, who himself was then the world famous editor of the Winnipeg Free Press with a high reputation as a political reporter.

After the collision, Mr.Roberton apologized and said in his deep Scottish brogue, "You look rather glum, Nick, as though you've lost your last friend!"

I replied that I was somewhat disappointed with Mr.Coo, and to make a long story short, I showed Mr.Roberton the picture.

"I'd like to keep this," he said, "I'll see what I can do about it!"

About two weeks later he called me into his office.

"Nick," he said, "about that picture. I showed it to Mr.Dafoe. He liked it very much

and so do I. We're going to run it on the editorial page next week!"

Well, the editorial page of the Free Press was sort of a sacrosanct area. Lowe, the famous English cartoonist, and our own equally famous Arch Dale were some of the few illustrators ever seen on the editorial page, never mind an unknown photographer. Now all of a sudden I'm handed something that I had never expected and it became, indeed, a turning point in my life. When the picture was published, there was very good reaction from the readers.

Mr.Dafoe was happy and Mr.Roberton called on me one day and said, "Nick, can you make more like this?"

I told him I thought I could, but it would be a full time job; you just can't get a picture like that every day. From that point on I never looked back!

I was given a Free Press automobile and went on to write a regular column entitled `Saturday Snapshots.' It ran on the letters to the editor page and was often filled with curious and strange phenomena.

For instance, a man came into the editorial room one day and asked for me. He had with him an ordinary spring onion that he had pulled out of his garden on a vacant lot in Winnipeg. The onion had seeded and grown up through a wedding ring that had initials on it. So I photographed it and ran it in my column with the story. If the owner wished to pick it up at the Free Press offices, he could do so by identifying the initials on the inside of the ring.

Two hours after the paper hit the streets we had a phone call from a gentleman who explained that his wife had lost a ring on a vacant lot at the exact corner where it had been found and that the initials were `AHBH.' He explained further that his wife had been running for a streetcar across the lot when she lost it, but it had never been found... That was the sort of thing I was running as a column - a general interest story line.

I was also then starting to produce pictures for the Toronto Saturday Night, which was of great prestige value, but paid little. Saturday

The ring with the onion that grew through it. NMC

Farmers haying along the Gaspe peninsula in Quebec. *NMC*

A classic photograph of British Columbia's renowned Okanagan orchards near Naramata, circa 1950. *NMC*

The native mission church at Chase, B.C., faced east overlooking Little Shuswap Lake. *NMC* 1954.

Canadian Pacific piers at the foot of downtown Vancouver in 1962. *NMC*

The Canadian Pacific Express terminal at Vancouver, B.C., and in the background the Sun newspaper building with the Woodwards building, festooned with the large "W," in the background. *NMC* 1962

Canadian Pacific's stately York Hotel in downtown Toronto, opposite Union Station. *NMC* 1955

The intersection of Front and Bay Streets looking north toward Toronto City Hall in 1955. Nick made the photograph from atop Union Station at midday. Note the Canadian Pacific Express trucks. *NMC*

Trucking was an important part of Canadian Pacific till the recent years of cutbacks. Smith Transport was an Ontario company that Canadian Pacific purchased in 1958.

Morant posed a Smith Transport International cab-over with pup trailers along a Northern Ontario highway for this beautiful fall photograph. *NMC*

Canadian Pacific also had heavy investments in logging on Vancouver Island through a company called Pacific Logging. In this photograph, Morant portrays high lead logging with a portable spar tree that drags the logs up out of the clear cuts to the landing where they are loaded on a Hayes tractor hauling 20 foot wide bunks. The photograph is near Cobble Hill, B.C., and was typical up till the 1980s when environmental concerns and the exhaustion of old growth forests brought drastic changes to the forest industry. *NMC*

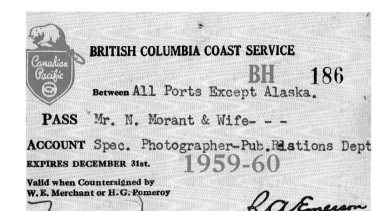

BRITISH COLUMBIA COAST SERVICE

BH 186

Between All Ports Except Alaska.

PASS Mr. N. Morant & Wife - - -

ACCOUNT Spec. Photographer-Pub. Relations Dept

EXPIRES DECEMBER 31st. 1959-60

Valid when Countersigned by
W. E. Merchant or H. G. Pomeroy

R A Emerson
Vice-President

Canadian Pacific

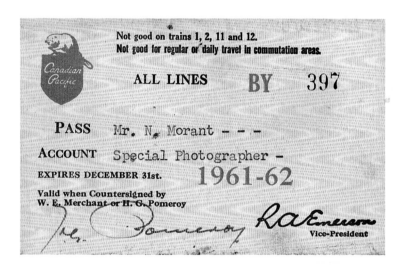

Not good on trains 1, 2, 11 and 12.
Not good for regular or daily travel in commutation areas.

ALL LINES BY 397

PASS Mr. N. Morant - - -

ACCOUNT Special Photographer -

EXPIRES DECEMBER 31st. 1961-62

Valid when Countersigned by
W. E. Merchant or H. G. Pomeroy

R A Emerson
Vice-President

Canadian Pacific
Canadien Pacifique

Not good on trains 1, 2, 11 and 12.
Not good for regular or daily travel in commutation areas.
Non valide sur les trains 1, 2, 11 et 12.
Non valide pour voyage régulier ou journalier en banlieue.

ALL LINES
TOUT LE RESEAU BY 0224

PASS
LAISSEZ-PASSER Mr. N. Morant - - -

ACCOUNT
TITRE Special Photographer -

EXPIRES DECEMBER 31st
EXPIRE LE 31 DÉCEMBRE 1965-66

VALID WHEN COUNTERSIGNED BY
VALIDE SI CONTRESIGNÉ PAR
H. G. POMEROY or/ou B. F. WALSH

GOOD OR FREIGHT TRAINS AND ENGINES

VICE-PRESIDENT · VICE-PRÉSIDENT

GOOD FOR PASSAGE ONLY — DOES NOT COVER MEALS AND BERTH

The person who accepts this Pass, thereby and in consideration thereof assumes all risks of accident and expressly agrees to make no claim upon the Company; and that the Company shall not be liable under any circumstances, whether of negligence by its servants or otherwise, for any injury to person, or for any loss or injury to the property of the person using this Pass; and that as to such person in the use of such pass the Company shall not be considered common carriers or liable as such.

The person to whom this Pass is issued is not prohibited by law from receiving free transportation and will lawfully use the same.

This Pass may be cancelled at any time, and presented by any other than the person named hereon will be taken up by the Purser and FULL FARE collected.

THIS PASS WILL NOT BE HONORED UNLESS SIGNED BY THE PERSON
WHOSE NAME APPEARS HEREON
SUBJECT TO CONDITIONS ENDORSED HEREON

CHAPTER FIVE
Back To The CPR - 1939.

Brushed aside by Victor Sifton, Nick Morant recalled Hugh Campbell's words of advice when he left the CPR in 1935... "Spend a few years on the newspaper, learn all you can, and undoubtedly you'll be able to come back to the CPR on your own terms."

So I got back to them, I sent a letter of application to Montreal saying that I'd like to rejoin the Company, and I visualized the sort of job I would have and how I could best serve the interests of the CPR.

Since Sir Edward Beatty, Chairman and President of Canadian Pacific, was most interested in better media coverage, an experienced press photographer on staff was thought to be what the Company needed for promotion and advertising. Morant was duly invited to Montreal to look over the photographic department.

Nick made known his enthusiasm to return, but at the same time adamantly insisted on one condition. He had to be allowed complete freedom from the confines of the photographic department itself. He hoped to avoid the morass of darkroom technicalities and the politics of interdepartmental demands. He required freedom from the traditional constraints of bureaucracy to produce the kind of photographs that the public relations and advertising people needed to further the Company's image. He proposed that he supply his own equipment and from his own darkroom he would submit the first set of prints from original negatives.

Management acceded to those conditions and Nick was assigned to the General Publicity Department (as the Public Relations Department was then called) under John Murray Gibbon, as "Special Photographer." As had happened years earlier when Nick was hired by the Free

Press, many hard feelings came from within the photographic department over this precedent. In time though, Morant smoothed things over with careful consideration and concern for those stuck in the darkrooms at Windsor Station.

Anticipating the challenge of working for the CPR once more, Morant resigned from the Free Press, giving no reason nor excuse for his departure. Some years later he encountered Victor Sifton in the dining room of the Royal York Hotel, surrounded by fellow newspaper and publishing people. Sifton recognized Morant and asked him, perhaps jocularly, if offered a higher wage than the CPR paid, would he not like to return to the Free Press? The gentlemen were left agape when Nick replied, *Thank you sir - but no - once was enough!*

E.W.Beatty was chairman and president of the CPR when Morant first started with the Company in 1929. He was still the head of the CPR when Morant returned in 1939, though a Knight of the Order of the British Empire since 1935. As fate would have it, Beatty's long tenure at the CPR was fortunate for Morant, as Sir Edward personally interceded on Nick's behalf when internal politics nearly put an end to his new job...

This story evolved around my return to the Company after working for the Free Press. My hiring was instantly opposed by a guy by the name of Norrish, who was the head man at the Associated Screen News. Inasmuch as a number of CPR men had invested in the Associated Screen News, it was more or less a CPR subsidiary. Norrish's company had, amongst other things, sole commercial rights for photography in the CPR hotels. This meant that they had a monopoly on the sale of scenic pictures and postcards in the newsstands and tourist shops of these hotels, as well as the rights to the amateur photo finishing that came

through the newsstands.

I knew nothing about this, Norrish didn't want any kind of interference at all in his monopoly of CPR territory, but there's a hell of a difference between a guy doing news and advertising pictures as compared to what Norrish was doing. I was hired to fill a large gap in CPR publicity. My work was not for sale to people in the hotels. One of the reasons I was hired was that Associated Screen News neglected to utilize the news photographer touch in their work. For instance, their photographs would show two people standing at a scenic location doing nothing. They didn't understand that what sold in those days were photographs of people engaged in some activity within the scenic surroundings, whether it be fishing, golfing, hiking, or any number of others. So there really never was any conflict, but it was surprising what happened next.

Norrish didn't go to John Murray Gibbon, the head of the General Publicity Department. He let it be known that he didn't think very much of this invasion and that he had every right to put an end to it. He went straight to Sir Edward Beatty. As Sir Edward was the head of the CPR, he was ultimately responsible for hiring me.

One day I was approached by Harry Smith, the manager of the General Publicity Department, who asked me, "Do you have any of your photographs on hand right now, stuff that is pretty?"

I replied, "No, why do you ask?"

So he told me what was going on.

"What I want you to do," he said, "is to drop everything, go grab some of your best pictures and fix them up any way you like. Then bring them back to me and I will show them to Beatty."

So I made up some pictures for Mr.Smith - really did them up so that Leonardo da Vinci had nothing on me!

Smith went up to Sir Edward's office, full

of the fear that Sir Edward managed to instill in all his subordinates, and said to him, "I thought that before we made any decisions here we should at least look at this man's work."

He went on to plead my case, explaining that we weren't doing anything to get in Norrish's way since we were not selling pictures to the public. Associated Screen News held those rights that the General Publicity Department respected, and besides, ASN's existing services were needed to do the publicity work.

Smith offered Sir Edward the portfolio that I had provided. Sir Edward glanced at them briefly saying, "They're very nice. Could you leave them here?"

Later the photographs were returned to Smith with a note attached saying, "Please see me."

Ten minutes later Smith was seated before the President. Sir Edward sat back in his chair and said, "You know Benny Norrish, he takes things too seriously some times. I can't see that he's going to be hurt one damn bit by this man and, as a matter of fact, I think Morant could teach the ASN boys a few tricks... and, said Beatty, I told him so, too!"

That was how Sir Edward saved my job, unknown to me, but it just shows you, the cards were on my side!

When I first worked for the CPR in 1929, people thought of Sir Edward Beatty as a God. He was aloof and all-powerful, in complete control of their destinies, so they believed. I remember the first time that air-conditioning was introduced in passenger cars; it was first tried on a Board of Directors' special train. Sir Edward was on that train when they brought it into Winnipeg. Everyone in the station was made to turn out on the platform upon its arrival. The train had been measured so that somebody signalled the engineer exactly where he should stop (this was simply a repeat performance for occasions when Royalty happened to come to town), placing Sir Edward right in front of the Vice President of Western Lines who stood at the head of this great long line of people arranged in their pecking order, according to their respective positions in the Company.

Sir Edward stepped down and greeted the Vice President, the General Manager and his assistants, then walked right by the rest of the

crowd and on down the stairs into the station, hardly giving anybody else a glance. It was a dreadful sight to see, and when they abandoned such presentations the Company showed great wisdom in doing so because it was a class thing if ever there was one. A more demeaning display of subservience and crass arrogance you never saw. For a man who happened to be a senior officer like Chief Draughtsman, for arguments sake, with 50 or 60 men working under him, being ordered out to stand in line according to pecking order, number 86 or whatever, and then the President just walking by without any acknowledgment was demeaning as hell.

What is interesting is that there was always the 'grand gesture.' But I think this did not come as an order-in-council from Sir Edward. Rather I envisage it as something dreamed up by 'sycophants' in Winnipeg. I can offer another anecdote that backs up this theory, a well known story around Calgary for years:

Colin Pratt, Manager of the Palliser Hotel around the 1930's assigned a couple of men to scrub down the front steps leading to the sidewalk - hands and knees stuff! He became so enthusiastic that he extended the chore to take in the entire street a little beyond the eastern end of the hotel's frontal limits. Need I tell you that the grand parade of the Board of Directors of the CPR marched a hundred yards or so in a state of cleanliness that rivalled the operating rooms at the Calgary General! By today's standards this would appear demeaning (i.e. the Welcoming Committee), but it was the end of the era of the BIG MEN in INDUSTRY... today you can see a Captain of Industry carrying his own bags out of the airport entranceway!

Another interesting set of circumstances about Sir Edward that comes to mind when Nick speaks of the Chairman and President of the railway, is the relationship Beatty had with his personal secretary, Kate Treleaven...

Apparently, Katie was more than just a secretary to Sir Edward. Kate was a lady who, along with her friend, Mrs. Hayter-Reid of Montreal, had a great deal to do with choosing the furniture for some of the larger CPR Hotels - when there was a refurbishing binge going

on. How they became involved, nobody is sure. In retrospect, many of these establishments had the same style decor. The Banff Springs, Chateau Frontenac, Place Viger, Hotel Vancouver and The Empress in particular, all had this imitation Jacobean furniture made by a first class manufacturer of antique replicas in Montreal.

There was some suggestion that the ladies were getting something in the way of remuneration, one of those things that no one could prove, but it was apparent what was going on. Mrs. Hayter-Reid's home in St.Andrews, New Brunswick became a showpiece - 'Pansy Patch' it was called... a 'Tudor Style' residence. There were carved wooden squirrels on garden gates and all in the best of taste. The house still stands in good repair directly across the street from the Algonquin Hotel... in the early days there was a 'colony' of homes associated with the CPR (at St.Andrews and also the Seigneury outside Ottawa), one of the prominent owners was the Hon.C.D.Howe, the wartime Supplies Minister in Ottawa during World War II.

Getting back to Katie though... she was a lady to be reckoned with, and was the only person I ever knew in Windsor Station (CPR's head offices) who had a dog sleeping beside her desk all the time. What exactly she did I could never tell, other than 'screening' people for Sir Edward. Whenever I passed by, she was always sitting there, reading a book!

I was just a budding photographer then, not getting anywhere fast, but able to take a half decent shot. I was assigned to get a picture of Sir Edward in Montreal, so I had to go see him. He had two private secretaries in the outer office, two men. Then you had Katie! She wanted to know all your business - why you where there. Particularly if you were a photographer!

Once past Kate, Sir Edward gave me a bit of trouble. He greeted me and we shook hands; at his bidding I took a seat in front of his big desk. Briefly we discussed where the photo was to be taken - in front of a large portrait of Lord Shaughnessy that hung in the Board Room.

"How long is this going to take - I can only give you ten minutes!" he said.

"Mr.Beatty," I replied, "if you've only got ten minutes for something like this that is as important to you as it is to me... I think we should pack it up for now and I'll come back at a more convenient time. I need a little longer to do your portrait justice."

"Well, where do we go?" said Sir Edward.

"I'm set up in the Board Room already, sir," I replied.

We were finished in fifteen minutes. The old man retired into the gloom of his office and I packed up and wondered if a twenty-fifth of a second at 5.6 was indeed the right exposure...

When I returned with the pictures, I got past the first two secretaries easily enough. I told them I had the 'old man's' photographs. When I encountered Miss Treleaven, she started one of her routine 'interrogations.'

Explaining that I had Sir Edward's pictures, she said, "Well, show them to me!"

Rather coolly, I replied, "You know, Miss Treleaven, it is customary that photographers never show pictures of their subjects to anybody but the principals themselves because they may not approve of what they see. I don't think I should make an exception here."

At that moment, totally by chance, Sir Edward came to the door.

"Oh," he said, "you've got the pictures. Bring them in!"

He was quite affable, seemed to like them, saying, "Well, that's fine."

The phone rang; I said, "Thank you, sir," and walked out. Miss Trealeven looked daggers at me as I passed her desk.

When Sir Edward died in 1943, Kate Treleaven was out of the office by noon that day. They practically pulled the carpets out from beneath her, much unloved was she!

Portrait of Sir Edward Beatty in front of the painting of Lord Shaughnessy in the CPR's board room, Windsor Station, Montreal, 1939. *NMC*

87

Steaming up the St.Lawrence River along the Montreal waterfront, the Empress of Canada passes beneath the Jacques Cartier bridge enroute to a berth after successfully navigating the Atlantic, circa 1950. *NMC*

Portfolio III

Ships

Empty "Lakers" ride high in the water along the
Neebing River, waiting to load grain at the N.M.Patterson
terminal in Port Arthur, Ontario, circa 1935. Morant stood on
a railway bridge over the river when he made the
photograph, with the Paterson boat Sarniadoc moored next
to the elevator waiting to load. *NMC*

In early morning fog, a "Laker" loaded with grain at Port Arthur, heads out into Thunder Bay and Lake Superior. The lake boats transhipped grain from the "Lakehead" to various ports on the Great Lakes and St.Lawrence River where the grain was loaded on ocean going ships for export. The ports of Fort William and Port Arthur, located adjacent to each other on the Ontario shore of Lake Superior were eventually amalgamated to become the City of Thunder Bay. *NMC*

At the CPR Pier in the Port of Vancouver, the <u>Empress of Russia</u> is reprovisioned for its retirn to Yokohama, Japan, circa 1935. NMC

Canadian Pacific ran coastal services along the inlets of
British Columbia and Vancouver Island from the time the
CPR was built till the 1970s. On the run from Vancouver to
Prince Rupert in the post war years, <u>Princess Adelaide</u> docks
at Prince Rupert after her overnight run from Vancouver,
circa 1948. *NMC*

A Matson Lines freighter leaves Active Pass heading for the Port of Vancouver. Willie stands on Galiano Island (one of the many Gulf Islands off the east shore of Vancouver Island) beneath an Arbutus tree looking across Active Pass toward Mayne island, circa 1963. *NMC*

<u>Beaverash,</u> a freighter owned by Canadian Pacific (Bermuda) Ltd.(established in 1964), was photographed on Lake Ontario in 1969 with the steel mills of Hamilton, Ontario in the background. *CPCA*

The first ship purchased by Canadian Pacific (Bermuda)
Ltd. was the R.B.Angus, photographed by Morant at
Chemainus, B.C. in 1965, loading lumber for export to Japan.
CPCA

An aerial view of Chemainus harbour made by Morant shows the R.B.Angus loading lumber. The ship was lost in a storm 620 miles off the coast of Japan in December 1967 with no loss of life. *CPCA*

Cruising in Alaskan waters, <u>Princess Patricia</u> slowly traverses Glacier Bay in the final assignment for this elegant ship in the late 1970s. *CPCA*

Wearing the CP Ships "multimark" on red stacks, <u>Princess Marguerite</u> nears the end of her career on the Victoria-Seattle summertime run, circa 1978. *CPCA*

"Canadian Mosaic" is a montage that Morant produced
in his darkroom, combining a photograph of the City of
Montreal with the famous Manitoba plowman photograph
from <u>Winnipeg Free Press</u> days. *NMC*

Part II

The War Years (1939 -1945)

Christian Haesler, a Swiss guide in the employ of the
CPR, stands on the shore of Sherbrooke Lake on the fateful
fall day in 1939 that he and Morant were attacked by the
female Grizzly bear. Cathedral Mountain looms in the
background. *NMC*

CHAPTER SIX
The Bear Story

From the time that Nick Morant rejoined the CPR in 1939, until 1945, the world became caught up in one of the greatest conflagrations man has known - World War II. This period of history became a time of great peril for any man of military age who volunteered or was draughted into the service of his country. In Nick's case, he was rejected by the military health authorities because of injuries suffered on September 19, 1939, when fate, in the form of a large female grizzly bear, struck at Morant and Swiss guide Christian Haesler.

Though still employed by the CPR, Morant was lent to the federal government and the National Film Board of Canada during the war years. He traveled extensively shooting material for government propaganda and information campaigns. Although this assignment, at first glance, seemed a mundane and sedentary part to play in the war effort, it proved to be as perilous as being on the front lines at times. In three instances during this period, fate intervened in Morant's life.

The first case was prior to his assignment to the National Film Board, and was his last assignment for the CPR till after the end of hostilities in 1945. Morant was severely wounded by a grizzly attack in Yoho National Park, and subsequently hospitalized for some time. His guide, Christian Haesler, also suffered serious wounds, wounds that led to his death and indirectly to the deaths of other members of his family. As this last statement implies, there were a number of bizarre twists to the bear story.

Edward Feuz, the senior member of the CPR's Swiss guides, was supposed to have accompanied Morant but Haesler went in his place. They were on assignment with the Canadian Pacific Hotels to search for a suitable location for a hikers' teahouse around Sherbrooke Lake, high in the Great Divide country. From Golden, they were to ride a freight train as far as Hector, B.C., on Wapta Lake, but Haesler lacked a pass to ride. A Superintendent from Revelstoke happened to be in Golden on his business car, so the problem was solved - a thousand to one chance for such a contact.

Sherbrooke Lake drains into the Kickinghorse River just below Wapta Lake. A crude trail led from Hector station up into the valley between Paget Peak and Mount Ogden that cradles Sherbrooke Lake. As Haesler and Morant headed north, animals were passing south, a normal fall occurrence they thought at the time. After the incident, the two men agreed that, had they not disregarded this indication of a bear in the area, the story might have had a different ending. Morant further relates that:

Since it might have been necessary to establish snow depths in the area, it was decided to take a five foot spruce, stripped down to use as a foot rule. Haesler swung it like a baseball bat and said, "First old grizzly we see we'll swipe him across the arse with this!" Thirty minutes later that's exactly what I was doing!

Further... prior to that fateful day, the whole scenario had been forecast by a friend of Nick and Willies', a lady who was something of a psychic, Jeannie Breithaupt. She had recently been assigned to the CPR's mountain hotels as a Press Relations officer. How this all came about is narrated by Morant in the following story...

My dear wife, Willie, and I resided in the Banff Springs Hotel during the summer season long before the development of the skiing craze that was to create a year-round business. A good deal of my time was given to covering other spheres of the CPR ventures such as coastal shipping, logging operations on Vancouver Island, the Empress Hotel in Victoria, and even some of the old sternwheeler operations on the inland lakes. A letter from the General Publicity Department instructed me to "Assist Miss Jean Alexander, our newly appointed press representative, by illustrating various stories she will be contributing in the course of her tenure at Banff."

Over the years I was to receive many such letters of instruction. I would always read between the lines for the real message. If the subject was an artist, for instance, I would know that somehow I must provide free transportation to a place where good compositions abounded and in an area we were promoting in our advertising campaigns. One of the many prominent persons that passed my way was the famous Canadian author, Hugh MacLennan. Knowing his love and sensitivity for the Canadian landscape, Willie and I took him to a remote section of the old Icefields Highway. Giving him a sandwich lunch and a thermos of coffee, we abandoned him beside a small lake. In three hours we returned to find him quietly surveying the great mountains around him. Later that day he was to return the favor by posing in a picture with Willie, beside the Athabasca Falls on a promontory that was later considered too dangerous to remain unfenced. This picture became a popular postcard - but nobody ever recognized who was in it.

On another occasion I was delegated to meet a very well known French journalist from Paris Soir. The Banff station platform was crowded with summer travellers as the passenger train arrived. Standing in the vestibule of a Pullman was a short gentleman with two cameras around his neck. He wore a beret, and carried an Air France flight bag. When he tipped his porter, I stepped forward and said, "Mr.Chamboureau?"

"Mais oui," he replied, "but how do you know me?"

We're a little off course here now, getting back to the story at hand... Jeannie came into our lives quietly, departing at season's end in her own unobtrusive style. She became our next door neighbor as we shared an unusual living space in the Banff Springs Hotel. The adjoining rooms, whose doors were less than five feet apart, were in the 'north tower,' somewhat of a landmark location. True, there were two flights of stairs to contend with, but once we reached our 'eagles nest' we could look downwards several hundred feet to the Bow Falls. Around us lay a magnificent unobstructed panorama of the valleys and surrounding peaks.

So it was we were launched into an entirely delightful friendship. It was but a fleeting encounter, spread over a few months. There were to be happy memories, but many of the principals involved were to face death and suffering before this tale unfolds.

For the present there were happy times. Everyone about us was young and everywhere there was an air of exuberance. For many of the staff, this was their first experience away from home - of being 'on their own' and enjoying the countless blessings afforded by a lack of parental restrictions. Troubles or grievous problems lay somewhere in a dim and distant future as yet unrevealed, even by fortune tellers.

Jeannie became a member of that happy society when she joined us in the 'tower.' She was to enter the lives of many youngsters: some advice here, a joke there, but she always kept her distance from their antics. No longer a teenager, she was 23! As Willie and I grew closer to her, we were able to become aware that there was a lot more to our Jeannie than first met the eye.

Along with friends, staff or guests, we all agreed that Jeannie Alexander was an outstanding personality. She had both beauty and talent. Her appearance in evening attire was regal, her deportment that of consummate grace. People would enquire of a bellboy, "Who is that stunning person?"

She was also a talented pianist, playing with feeling and finesse. Occasionally, just after midnight when the boys in the 'Big Band' had finished playing the last waltz in the ballroom, we would go down to the quiet and deserted Mount Stephen Hall, a lovely period suite with stained glass windows and little writing desks hidden away in quiet nooks. There Jeannie would join us, perching on the bench at the keyboard of the Heintzman Grand. She would play excerpts from classical or popular music of the day. Between numbers she would carry on little conversations with her audience, which seldom exceeded a dozen people. Not everybody shared the secret of these midnight concerts. I often wondered how many of the guests, tucked away in their beds in luxury suites upstairs, would have loved to have joined this clandestine audience if only for the half hour the concert lasted!

The lady was also a brilliant conversationalist, a talent that was to serve her well when seeking interviews with prominent guests. This was an era in the history of these hotels when actors and actresses from Hollywood and the New York stage would suddenly appear in the lobby or on the first tee of the golf course. One of these was Jack Benny, a leading American radio comic whose Sunday evening shows captivated the nation and embraced an entire continent. He turned up one evening with a group of friends and business associates along with the inevitable public relations man. The arrival of such a popular star meant that some good publicity was fruit on the vine, waiting to be plucked. True, we would be capitalizing on his presence in a CPR hotel and encroaching on his personal vacation time. However, this was the name of the game. Any actor knows that when you are left alone it must be that your popularity might just be slipping a wee bit!

Jeannie quickly made arrangements with the Benny press agent for an interview and what is now called a 'picture opportunity,' which was my responsibility. There was a problem, however. Jeannie was given to understand that Mr.Benny was golfing with friends and the most she could expect was a five minute interview.

That year, Benny had staged a number of skits on his radio show involving 'the old west' in a nonsensical classic known as 'Buck Benny Rides Again.' I had talked with the press agent and outlined my idea for a 'gag shot.' Benny would join an Indian Chief in full eagle feather costume on the back of a white horse. The actor would be waving a cowboy hat in the traditional stance of the western buckaroo.

The idea was quickly approved and the following afternoon found me on the golf course waiting, as it were, for the shoot out. With me was Jacob Two Young Man, a chief of the Stoney Tribe, who cut quite a dashing figure astride his old gray mare. Willie was on hand as always on such assignments, bringing with her a cowboy hat and step-ladder to facilitate the transfer of Mr.Benny to his assigned position on the horse, directly behind Jacob.

I sensed somehow that things were not going according to plan. After twenty minutes Mr.Benny still hadn't shown up. Meanwhile, problems were developing on the set. Jacob was anxiously inquiring in a low voice about the location of the nearest toilet facility. Further, in his own way of saying things, I gathered that it would be a case of too far to late were he to go to the facility on the seventh fairway. The old mare, as if to emphasize the situation, had committed an indiscretion on the fairway nearby.

When 40 minutes had elapsed from the agreed upon time, I decided to seek out Jeannie, Mr.Benny, or the press agent, up at the hotel. Leaving Willie in charge, with instructions to hold the actor until I returned, forcibly if necessary, I went to the room where the interview was to be staged for 'five minutes.' Just outside were some of the Benny entourage and the press agent who appeared on the verge of apoplexy. At the far end of the room was Mr.Benny, sitting tete-a-tete with Miss Alexander. They appeared to be blithely unconscious of the world outside. Anticlimatically, the 'gag photo' was eventually made and later published widely. Even today, as I look back into this little bit of history, the person who was captivated by this interview surely was Mr.Jack Benny - he of the cheapskate characterization, with the off-key attempts at playing 'The Bee' on an Amati fiddle.

The fact was that I knew very little about Jean Alexander, except that she had once lived in Calgary before marriage, later moving to Scarborough Heights in Toronto. She had left behind an infant with her husband and grand parents when she came out to Banff. It seemed she had impulsively accepted the offer of a public relations assignment for the summer before having to give up her career to become a fulltime mother. It was to be this little child in far off Toronto who would inadvertently reveal to us an altogether new and strange facet of the extraordinary personality of our new press agent.

Several weeks after Jeannie had settled into her quarters in the 'tower,' Willie and I were awakened from a deep sleep by someone pounding on our door. It was so insistent, this knocking, it sounded almost frantic in its beat. There stood our usually calm mannered associate. She was crying and wringing a small lace hankie, wet with tears. Willie got out of bed and tried to soothe her and find out what was wrong. I recall the time was ten minutes after four in the morning.

Slowly we learned that her little one was dangerously ill. "I'm afraid my child is going to die, Willie," she ventured.

We talked things over for about 15 minutes when I noticed she became a bit more relaxed. It was a noticeably sudden change.

Then Willie asked her, "How did you get this news, did someone phone? A telegram then - a letter?"

Jeannie looked at her and replied with child-like simplicity, "Willie dear, I just know these things."

Shortly afterward, a telephone call to her home in Toronto revealed that the child was with her father at a nearby hospital emergency ward. They had been last informed that the attack had been checked and the child was out of danger. That was just about the time when Jeannie so noticeably started to settle down.

She thanked us for our support, smiled at Willie and said, "I think I'll try a little more sleep."

The matter was never discussed again. It seemed obvious we were next door neighbors to someone endowed with psychic powers.

Halfway through the season one day, I joined Willie, who was having afternoon tea with Jeannie at the old Banff Springs golf clubhouse. Shortly after I arrived, two men appeared at the doors of the dining room and waited for a table. One of them was well known to Willie and me as an oldtimer with public relations, so we asked them to join us. The man we knew was Duncan McMurray. It was apparent that neither he nor Jeannie had met before, nor had she met the other man, whom McMurray introduced with a ficticious name as Mr.Johnson. It was a happy enough gathering, some fun here and there, but perhaps a bit laboured socially. At times Jeannie would be asked 'to do teacups' more as a party diversion than anything else. She regarded this with a jaundiced eye, saying to me once, "How can one read tea leaves when they're all in bags?'

She would deliberately move tea cups to one side, leaving them aside in disdain. It appeared that she was trying to disassociate herself from anything that suggested she was a tea cup reader. Her 'fortunes' for party purposes were pretty much the flippant, standard stuff, involving travel to distant lands, with mystic handsome men waiting at the end of the ship's gangplank to make off into the desert retreat with every available girl on board. So it was that she was asked 'to do tea cups' that afternoon. It proved to be a memorable and unusual seance. Certainly it wasn't fortune telling. Was it a demonstration of some form of telepathy then?

It was quickly decided that McMurray would be 'read' first. Fixing him with a steady gaze for a full minute, she slowly reached across the table and picked up a salt shaker. "Can I put it here - is that okay with you?"

He nodded absently and watched this time as she reached for the pepper pot holding it midair in the manner of a chess player uncertain of a move.

"Now," she chattered in the manner of an old woman at a fish market, "where in the world shall we find a home for this? Maybe here? But no - you wouldn't want it there now would you?"

Obviously she was teasing him and I think he knew this. He settled with her finally, with the shakers about eighteen inches apart. The next move involved the silver CPR sugar bowl, that she held by both handles. For a split second I pictured her in the role of a goddess at an altar in a Grecian temple! It was apparent that this was to be her 'piece de resistance.' Again the bantering talk and again the problem of placement - of where the hell it should go in order to please McMurray! 'Trying him out' as it were, she carried the bowl to a point about three inches from one of the shakers. McMurray smiled at her, as if he knew she shared his secret.

"Mr.McMurray," she said, "whatever it is you do depends entirely upon where you placed that sugar bowl!"

To those of us who knew the man, she had just painted his portrait.

Now her attention turned to the 'stranger in our midst' who had appeared to be engrossed by what he witnessed. For a few seconds she gazed at him in silence. She seemed to be sizing him up, or was this an 'adversary approach?'

"Would you mind," she said, "if I pour a little tea into your saucer?" This done, she asked him for his right hand and, as all watched, the tea was directed to the far side of the saucer. The entire procedure was repeated, but this time using his left hand. Again, the tea sought the new level created by the movement of his other hand.

I noticed Duncan McMurray shaking his head slowly as if in disbelief. As quickly as it all started - it was finished. But there was a brief epilogue.

"Sir," she said, "I would just say, that whatever it is you do involves a power of command you somehow exert in directing the flow of liquids in whatever direction you please... in just the manner you did with the tea in your saucer!"

With that, she pushed her chair away from the table, folded her hands in her lap and smiled sweetly at us all.

At this juncture, to be fair with my readers it is imperative that I digress, if but briefly, to provide an historical background of an era in southern Alberta during the 1920s. This will furnish a commentary that directly bears on that afternoon tea session in the Golf Clubhouse at Banff. There is a very old maxim that perhaps epitomizes the talents of this lady: "She who can see through a millstone."

As everyone knows, Canadian railway builders were encouraged by government to accept extensive land grants bordering their right of ways. This was a sort of down payment, or incentive to build, you might say, since no government could foot the bill in those days. Throughout the twenties Canadian Pacific was promoting the sale of their lands in western Canada by advertising throughout Europe, the British Isles and the USA, prompting a vigourous emmigration movement to Canada. They had plenty of competition because other railroads and the government were engaged in similar promotions. Canadian Pacific had its own Department of Natural Resources, as well as the independent Canada Colonization Association. Serving these and all other departments was the General Publicity office in Montreal. Every available advertising venue was utilized beyond newspaper and magazine announcements. One of these was the production of exhibition pieces that today would be referred to as `visual aids.' A typical exhibit, and there were hundreds of them varying in size from five feet to fifty feet, would feature agricultural products of the area involved. There was usually a banner displayed over the top portion, such as `Build Your Nest in the West.' Below this and balanced nicely, would be two large glass containers filled with samples of apples, pears, peaches, in a preservative solution. In absolute dead visual center would be an idealistic sheaf of wheat - created by workmen one stalk at a time, which required hundreds of hours of patient craftsmanship to complete. The salient feature of all these exhibits was that of absolute symmetry. They were indeed masterpieces of the era even if there were always some wags ready to say that the fruit displays in the preserving jars strangely resembled examples of diseased human organs soaking in formaldehyde in the backrooms of the medical schools. A workshop producing exhibits was located by the General Publicity people in Montreal. However, in the case of these very specialized agricultural exhibits, it was decided to locate a branch shop in Alberta (the Exhibits Branch of the Department of Immigration and Colonization of the CPR, which later became the Public Relations Department), closer to sources of the necessary material. The new shop was located on land a mile north of Canadian

Pacific's famed `experimental' dairy farm at Strathmore. The idea behind this project (and twelve others across Canada) was to offset criticisms concerning the viability of certain types of agriculture production in given areas. Strathmore farm had a prize winning herd of some 170 Holsteins, many of which were top butterfat producers and one of which was three times Grand Champion at the Chicago Fair. In 1924 this farm, beyond the dairying department, produced five hundred thousand pounds of poultry and three and a half million eggs, most of which ended up in CPR hotels and dining cars.

On the nearby prairie lands around Bassano and Brooks, Canadian Pacific was engaged in the development of a huge irrigation scheme. At the time this became the largest such project on the North American continent. There still stands an aqueduct a mile and a half long that in some places has arches as high as 50 feet.

So now we can assess Jeannie's abilities in the matter of her performance at the Banff Springs golf clubhouse. Duncan McMurray was for many years (1932 - 1947) Superintendent of the Exhibits Branch that built the symmetrical exhibits and who at times himself worked on the hand crafted wheat sheaves. You ask about the 'unknown stranger?' Need I tell you? At the time of our story, he was chief engineer in charge of the Bassano Irrigation project!

Who says, "you can't see through a millstone?"

Then one day it came my turn to face Jeannie on her home turf. Again, it was the afternoon tea party in the clubhouse! It was early September of 1939, and soon the hotel would be closed for the season. There were four of us: Jeannie's guest, Miss Ferguson, sister of the editor of the Montreal Star and the two inseparables - Willie and Nicholas.

I have little recall concerning earlier details of this meeting, but for some reason Jeannie offered to bring me up to date about the 'state of the nation,' as she put it. A minute later and I felt I wished she had kept quiet. Almost on the instant her voice changed and I felt she was

becoming emotionally disturbed.

"Nicky," she said, "there's an accident on a trail somewhere - not too far from here I think. I don't see anything of Willie but there's a man here... he's double your age and is very much involved in all this."

That was all she volunteered, but after tea she cornered me for a few seconds. Laying a hand on my arm, she looked at me with those earnest gray eyes of hers. They were filled with tears.

"Nicky," she implored, "please God will you be careful!

From that moment on, though I was unaware of it, I was being borne along by 'Hurricane Fate.' A date had already been set and inexorably we would all arrive 'on time.' It was to be September 19, 1939.

The account of the grizzly incident was well documented after the fact, although nearly every article written was grossly exaggerated, sensationalized and a fabrication of the truth. These stories made Christian Haesler the experienced guide and Nicholas Morant, a then well known outdoor photographer, look foolish indeed. Despite police evidence to the contrary, the stories gave the impression that Morant had been taking pictures of the bear when the attack occurred. Because of the wounds inflicted by the bear, Morant was never able to open his pack to get his first aid kit; the Graflex camera was still at the bottom of the closed pack when rescuers arrived. So, to throw off all the conjecture and false impressions, Morant anonymously wrote an article for Sports Afield giving the firsthand truth of the entire incident...

I decided to write the damn thing my own way. I didn't want to embarrass the CPR, but at the same time Haesler the guide, and I, were suffering at the hands of those idiots and it wasn't justified.

Here we recount, then, from the pages of Sports Afield, Nick Morant's harrowing escape from 'Hurricane Fate' and the predictions of Jeannie:

"We made one mistake," said Morant. "We trusted a grizzly. If we had walked the trail in fear it would have been a different story."

"Y'see," continued the photographer, as the guide, Haesler, quietly sucked away at his pipe before the fireplace, "Chris and I saw that bear first about 125 yards dead ahead of us and, if we'd been afraid, we'd have had lots of time to hit for a tree. But we just stopped for a moment, passed a few remarks about her and, as the old bear and the cub edged off to the left up a rock slide as they'll most always do, we continued on up the trail."

Mr. Morant pointed out that all the facts and figures mentioned are to be found in Royal Canadian Mounted Police reports and are not the result of collaboration between the two men after the accident. Neither saw the other until after their statements had been taken. That they had no guns was because they had passed through a National Park en route to where they were engaged in a photographic survey.

Let no sportsman wisely wag his head when he learns the silvertip had a cub with her. It never left the mother's side and both men were recognized as being too experienced to have come between the two.

As the grizzly edged off, along the side hill to the left, the cub went right along with her. As quickly as she climbed, she continued in her original direction until she had reached a point some 100 yards away, 50 feet above the men - with a creek between and her cub on the up-side of the hill. In a moment she was behind them and still climbing till they practically had forgotten her.

"The next thing I remember," said Morant, "was looking up at Chris, walking in front of me and seeing him suddenly glance back at the hill side. Never shall I forget the look on his face. A moment later I had glanced in that direction, instinctively finding the spot where last we had seen the two animals. The cub was there but not the mother. In a flash, half way down the rock slide, I could see the old mother - a silver grey streak as she came after us."

"Run for a tree," yelled Chris, throwing off his rucksack as he went.

"I shall never forget that race as long as I live. We ran like things possessed, expecting at any moment to be struck down from behind by that snarling beast. I remember thinking to myself that if I was to have half a chance to get into a tree (just try climbing a spruce sometime) I would run further into the bush, out of her sight. She would go after the first one she saw, I knew. This proved to be true - she caught poor Chris by the ankle when his feet were ten feet off the ground. He came down pulling the spruce boughs out in his hands - green ones too."

By now Nicholas Morant had reached a place of safety in his tree and it was his act of leaving this tree to attack the crazed silvertip that received such widespread publicity in the press from coast to coast. It was a case of a natural question arising, which any sporting man might well ask himself. "What would you have done if you had been sitting in that tree?"

"I could see the bear tearing at Chris and heard his awful cries. It made me wonder what to do - should I climb down or should I wait till she left him? If I came down - it was suicide. Yet, just the same, there was my good friend being torn to pieces in front of me. I had no arms of any kind - so I climbed down anyway, damn good and scared, picked up a stick (the one they had cut just before) about four feet long, and went over and whacked the old bear in the behind."

"She let out an awful roar, turned on me with her teeth showing, blood from Chris' wounds dripping from her jaws. With one jab of her front paws she knocked the stick out of my hands and the next moment she was after me."

Morant went on to describe how he remembered what his father, an old game warden had told him about the risks of 'standing up to a bear' - the danger of being swiped at by their gigantic front paws. With one blow they can crush a man's head like an eggshell. Let the reader, sitting in his home or lodge, pause a moment to realize what a frightening situation this must be. Unarmed - tackling a half ton beast that could pull a man out of a tree at ten feet with its mouth (remember - grizzlies can't climb trees).

"Well," said Morant, "I knew I'd get my block knocked off if I continued running - so I threw myself down on the ground and resolved to fight it out on my back. In a moment she was at me. I could see that big head, the little pig eyes, those three inch fangs and hear that awful roar that would scare anybody - I don't care how brave he might be. As she went at me I kicked her in the face but she came right on. I punched her in the face in a frenzy of fear and then I felt the most awful pain. [She broke his leg in two places, drilled a hole shown by x-rays almost the size of a .22 caliber bullet right through his leg - editor.] Next thing she came at my face again and I socked her as hard as I could - screaming like a madman. She took me by the right arm, above the elbow, with a roar and shook me like a puppy does a sock. Fear and pain nearly drove me out of my mind. I fought hopelessly with her, but she bit a hole in my arm - completely paralyzing it, before she let go."

Haesler thinks he must have been unconscious after her first attack on him. Reconstructing the occurrence, it is believed that the bear left Morant and came after the guide - biting him among other places, at the base of his spine - miraculously missing vital vertebrae.

Morant's narrative continues: "After she left me I managed to get up - feeling hopelessly exhausted. Driven by fear I managed to hobble across the clearing to a tree some 30 feet from where she'd left me. I had an idea to climb it, but realized this was impossible with a paralyzed arm. So I just stood there, breathing hard, bleeding terribly from the arm and leg, hoping to escape her notice. In a few moments she came tearing past me and let out an angry growl when she found I'd gone. She swung about and came straight for my tree - stopping right on the opposite side of it. I could easily have touched her hindquarters with my hand, she was that close. It was hide and go seek - only pretty grim business here. I didn't have to wait long - she must have smelled or heard me breathing. With a roar she was on me."

The photographer described the second assault. A nightmare it must have been - probably lasting but a very few moments. Morant was bitten in the hand and his left forearm muscle was nearly severed in a five inch cut. In making a reconstruction of the event, the men believe that whilst the second attack on Morant was going on, Haesler recovered consciousness. His forearm was badly mauled - a number of tendons and ligaments being torn out completely. Both his legs were stripped to the bone and muscle near the ankles and he quickly realized there was nothing he could do. He did what any outdoor man would agree was the wisest move. He went for aid. Fighting off unconsciousness at every step he half ran, half walked seven miles of mountain trail to the nearest warden's cabin to get help. Arrived there, his only interest was in the other man's welfare - before they called an ambulance to meet the party at the nearest road, he kept repeating - "Go look for my friend, quick, go look for my friend."

Mr.Morant then described how the grizzly came at him for a fourth time and would most certainly have killed him had it not been for the cub which yelped and called her away at the critical moment.

The photographer's return to civilization, after a brief search for Haesler, (who of course had already made his escape) is an amazing record. The bear went to the trail that lay between him and civilization, thus bottling him in the far end of the valley. Knowing it would have been suicide to go down the trail and risk another encounter, he decided on making a circle, to pick up the trail lower down. To do this he had to climb more than a thousand feet up the mountain side and walk four miles along precipitous cliff and rock slopes, descending another thousand feet to reach the valley floor again.

Searchers sent out by the valiant Haesler found him, a "terrifying bloody object - but still on his feet fighting his way back to civilization."

Following a 56 mile journey in a forestry truck, he reached hospital where doctors placed 32 'drains' in his various wounds. He was out in the wilds, badly wounded, from approximately 9am till 6.30pm when he was found by the search party - he did not reach the hospital until nearly midnight.

Such is the story of one of the few men who ever attacked a silvertip unarmed and lived to tell the tale.

Jim Coleman, Morant's school chum from University School, a well known newspaper columnist, once summed up the entire episode when he wrote an article introducing Nick and Willie and their slide show, 'A Talk Without Words':

"A national magazine once asked me to write a piece on 'memorable meals' which I had enjoyed," wrote Coleman. "I declined to write the piece, on the reasonable grounds that the meals which I recall most vividly were only those meals which had been memorably lousy.

"If I had given a bit of sober thought to the magazine's request, I had a story with a reverse twist. I could have written about the occasion on which Nicholas E. Morant was served up, in person, as a meal for a grizzly bear.

"Although I have had many strange friends, Nick Morant is the only one of those friends to have been eaten by a grizzly. Fortunately, Morant was a singularly indigestible fellow - stringy and tough - and, when the bear left the table temporarily, looking for some soda-bicarbonate or a package of Tums, Morant managed to escape. But, he spent many months in hospital while the plastic surgeons carefully filled the cavities in his limbs and torso.

"Those grizzlies always forget to replace their divots.

"Nick Morant who has survived many nutty experiences to become one of the world's finest scenic photographers, was sitting in my office recently, briefing me on his latest escapades. Turning back the conversational clock, more than 20 years, I asked if he had any particular vivid recollection of his encounter with the grizzly.

"'Yes,' he replied solemnly. 'I remember that the bear had a serious case of halitosis.'"

Portfolio IV

Banff Indian Days and the North

With Willie assisting, Morant makes a portrait of a
Stoney Indian chief on the Morley Reserve west of Calgary.
b It is interesting to note his use of fill-in-flash, a technique
that has recently seen a great resurgence amongst leading
photographers. *NMC*

A portrait of a Stoney chief at Banff Indian days wearing a medal that is inscribed in a foreign language with the year 1864 and what appears to be a "Hapsburg Eagle" in the center. The Stoney Indians were a western tribe of the Assiniboines, who themselves were Siouan or Dakota people. *NMC*

In all their finery, a family of the Stoney tribe poses for Morant in front of their tipis, Cascade Mountain looms in the background. Banff Indian Days first took place in 1889, instigated by Tom Wilson for guests at the CPR's Banff Springs Hotel, and was an annual event up until 1978. *NMC*

At Dawson City in the Yukon, a "sourdough" poses on the shore of the Yukon River in front of the sternwheeler <u>Klondike</u> in 1947. *NMC*

In 1942, Morant was assigned by the Canadian
Government to photograph the construction of the Alaska
Highway. Along the way he made pictures of the narrow
gauge White Pass and Yukon Railway that ran from
Skagway, Alaska, over the White Pass to Whitehorse in the
Yukon Territory. This famous railway photograph is of
Hurricane Gulch and shows a mixed train led by a US Army
2-8-2 locomotive bound for Whitehorse, crossing the spindly
bridge, climbing toward the White Pass. *CPCA*

In a later era, near Bennett in British Columbia, Morant photographed the colorful Yukon and White Pass tourist trains that carried cruise ship patrons from Skagway to Bennett and back in the 1970s. The locomotives are custom built General Electric units powered by Alco 251 diesels of about 860hp. Many of the passenger cars are original, built for the railway when it was completed in 1900. *CPCA*

At Tagish, Yukon Territory, Morant photographed the sternwheeler <u>Tutshi</u> at her moorings. The sternwheeler era was coming to an end as implicated by the beached vessel in the background, but in the summer of 1947, you could still travel up and down the Yukon waterway by riverboat. *CPCA*

CHAPTER SEVEN
The Sequel

Jeannie had forecast what turned out to be the bear accident. She did not know nor had she ever thought it would be a bear, only that there was to be an accident, that something was about to happen on a trail and that there was to be another man involved older than Morant. She had once told Nick, "...teacups, tarot cards, ordinary everyday playing cards, and all the fortune telling gimmicks mean nothing; it's what you feel about the person that counts." So there is a sequel to this story, perhaps more than one, as recounts Morant...

When I was on the train one day going back to Montreal, I was walking through the sleeping cars when a man in one of the drawing rooms of the train shouted out, "Nick, hey Nick!" I stopped and went back. It was Mr.Paterson, owner and president of Paterson Grain Elevators and the Paterson grain shipping fleet.

I must digress again, to tell you that I had known Mr.Paterson from an earlier venture that he had some time ago in connection with the CPR. He had decided to promote skiing in Fort William in the early days, and since he was a big shipper with the CPR, he approached the railway for help in the promotion of his venture. He had put up all the money for the project but needed publicity to try to make it a self-supporting project.

So Mr.Paterson recognized me as I was walking by, since I had worked with him when he had come into the CPR's publicity department for help. He was by himself in the drawing room. In those days all the important and wealthy people travelled in drawing rooms or bedrooms on first class passenger cars. Today a business man would never see a railway train; he'd be flying first class. When I sat down with Paterson, he immediately asked me about the bear...

He had read all about the accident, which had happened about 18 months earlier, and asked if I would mind telling him first hand what

happened, since he had heard so many conflicting stories. I told him the entire bear story in detail.

We had lots of time, and when I had finished and he was remarking on it, I said, "You know, equally unusual was the fact that the whole damn thing was forecast in a reading by a fortune teller."

Without hesitation, he said, "I know who that would be - Jean Alexander."

Paterson sat back and proceeded to tell me a story of his own: "I was travelling east on this train some four or five years ago, with a business associate. We were going down to New York City and just as we are sitting here now with the door open, two girls went by, one of whom my friend knew. He called her by her first name and invited both to join us. Tea was ordered.

We were sitting around chatting, and as we finished our tea, the girl my associate knew spoke up and said that her friend, Jeannie, could read teacups. `Let's have a reading!' she insisted.

Instantly, I sensed Jeannie wanted no part of it, for she fought it very pleasantly and said, `No, I'm rather tired, and if you don't mind please, I'd rather not.'

Paterson's travelling companion suggested; `At least read your friend's teacup!'

Jeannie acquiesced and gave a reading after which the other girl insisted on more. `Aw, come on, do another, at least this gentleman's.'

You could just see that she was at the breaking point. Suddenly she burst into a flood of tears, got up, nearly knocking the tray off the table, and ran out the door with her face in her hands. That was the end of the party.

My associate dropped dead in New York City four days later. Apparently he had no future to read!"

That was the little adventure into the psychic that I experienced, or had heard of, in connection with this woman. I was talking to her at lunch in the Royal York Hotel one day and

for a brief moment this same story came up, brought about by my mention of Paterson's name.

I inquired of her, "Jeannie, did you know that that gentleman was going to die, did you know that he had no future?"

And even then, 20 years after the event, tears came into her eyes and she said, "Nicky, a lot of these so called talents aren't all they're cracked up to be!"

A second sequel lay in the events that overtook Christian Haesler, the guide, and his family, in the years just prior to and following the bear accident.

Golden, British Columbia, was a quiet mountain town in 1937, when one fall afternoon an explosion blew apart the basement of the home of Ernest Feuz, Swiss mountain guide.

Fred Feuz, son of Ernest, was re-building a guitar by the light of a coal-oil lamp when the youngest son of Christian Haesler came into the basement. Haesler's son, Bill, was a reckless 14-year-old who was always getting into some kind of mischief, but usually survived any predicament, the blame often falling on his older brother, Walter.

Bill came into the basement with a little sack in his hand, an old rag filled with red powder. He said, "look what I've got - let's make a firecracker!" Fred wasn't interested in firecrackers - he wanted to finish his guitar. Bill looked around in a box full of scrap metal where he found a pipe into which he began tamping the powder. Fred stood there watching with his guitar, the coal-oil lamp flickering in the dark cellar, when all of a sudden - wham!

The explosion knocked Fred down and apparently blasted a piece of metal into young Haesler's chest. Total darkness

NMC

A Stranraer flying boat passes overhead of the light at
Peggy's Cove, Nova Scotia, in a photograph made by Willie
during the Second World War. *NMC*

One of Canada's most famous places, Peggy's Cove in Nova Scotia, portrayed through the camera of Nicholas Morant. Note the artist with his easel on the rocks to the left of the harbor entrance. *NMC*

It is Exhibition Days at Lunenburg Harbor as the signal
flags are snapping in the wind on the schooner <u>Bluenose II</u>
and <u>Lightship No.2.</u> *NMC*

Mists drift through the masts of the schooner <u>Ronald
Cloughmire</u> in Lunenburg Harbor, 1950. *NMC*

Reprovisioning the <u>Ronald Cloughmire</u> for another
fishing expedition to the Grand Banks. *NMC*

Centreville Cove, Nova Scotia. *NMC*

Woods Harbor, Nova Scotia. *NMC*

128

Blue Rocks, Nova Scotia. *NMC*

129

131

During the Second World War, Canadian Pacific's Angus Shops in Montreal became a military tank factory as well as a locomotive shop. To illustrate the railway's war effort, Morant made this photograph from the roof of the shop building looking down on tanks receiving finishing touches prior to shipping overseas, and locomotive No.2801, an H1A class 4-6-4 fresh from re-building. The photograph was made specially for <u>Fortune Magazine.</u> *NMC*

CHAPTER EIGHT

On "Civvy" Street : World War II

Recovery from the wounds of the grizzly bear took time. World War II was well under way, Europe was over run by Hitler's Nazis; defeat of the Allies and invasion of England seemed imminent. Only the valiant air war in British skies -the Battle of Britain - held any hope for the defense of England. More decisive, but less dramatic, was the Battle of the Atlantic - to supply England with the necessary materials and supplies to overcome the Nazi threat. From the beginning, Canadian volunteers flooded the Royal Air Force. From Halifax, large convoys of merchant ships, protected by Royal Navy and Royal Canadian Navy anti-submarine escorts, set out for England. Canada was involved from the start, and the lifeline of men and material ensured British survival, though the cost in ships and men was astronomical as the German U-Boats attempted to stem the flow.

Nicholas Morant tried to join the war effort, as did so many young Canadians, but the Navy, to whom he applied to serve as a photographer, declared him unfit to serve because of injuries received in the grizzly bear accident. The man who got the job was a friend of Nick's named Gerry Richardson, an outstanding feature photographer for the Toronto Star...

I knew Gerry very well as I worked on the Royal Tour of 1939 with him. He got the job I had applied for in the Navy and eventually came out as a Lieutenant-Commander, which wasn't a bad ranking for a guy who was officially a photographer. When he joined, his rank was Sub-Lieutenant and he had to take orders from just about everyone out there; they'd all tell him where he could or couldn't take pictures and so he received almost no on the job co-operation at all.

On one occasion, he told me, when he first started, he realized what he had gotten himself into when he asked a gunnery officer if he would traverse two of his guns over to the right (starboard) about 20 degrees so that he could get a picture of the convoy underneath the protecting guns of the Canadian Navy - a logical and important shot, one that everybody would want to use. The gunnery officer looked him up one side and down the other; a sub-lieutenant just simply did not ask a gunnery officer a favor in the Navy! In other words, he'd run head on into a Reserve man. They were not like the easy-going volunteers that had joined the fight and who were far more informal. Gerry had a difficult time of it all through the war. Perhaps I was spared the problems as it was determined that I was unfit to serve...

I was now on 'civvy' street. It turned out that the Department of Public Information in Ottawa needed a photographer, so I was loaned by the CPR for such services as long as it was necessary. I was the only photographer at first ... I did everything.

The Department of Public Information (DPI) had existed for some years. Its purpose was to produce polished information concerning government activities. As Canada became embroiled in World War II, the Dominion Government created a new agency entitled the Wartime Information Board, and appointed Charles Vining, a man long associated with the newspaper business, as its leader. The government quickly merged the DPI into the War Information Board and it was in 1941 that Morant joined the team as its photographer.

Later, the government took on another of Canada's top photographers, Harry Rowed. He was a long time friend and competitor of Morant. The two photographer's became known around Ottawa as the "Glammer Boys," partly for the natty way they dressed, but more perhaps, for the way they made exciting photographs out of the most mundane subjects.

Finally, a third man joined the team, Ronny Jaques, from the Stills Division of the National Film Board; a man who even at the age of 80 and older, travelled the world of expensive resorts, restaurants and tourist locations on assignment for the international glamour magazine Gourmet. As a team, the three men created a pictorial record of more than 15,000 negatives of Canada at war.

The National Film Board, that served as a government agency under the direction of John Grierson, formed its "Stills and Graphics Division" in 1942, and it was into this organization that the Wartime Information Board folded. The staff of the Wartime Information Board and the Stills Division went on operating under the NFB name as though nothing had changed. They worked well under a gentleman by the name of Ralph Foster who had ability and drive, but lacked the usual Ottawa career pushiness.

John Grierson, a charismatic Scot, was an outspoken critic of Canadian movie production who became Canada's first Film Commissioner. For reasons unknown, he gained the sobriquet "Birdlegs," but it is a fact that throughout Morant's working life associates around him have picked up nicknames that usually stick because of their oddball innocence.

Morant and Rowed worked well together. They were both farm boys, and worked on rival newspapers in Winnipeg at the same time. They often co-operated with each other on mundane assignments, unknown to their editors, unless of course one could scoop the other on an important event. Both photographers loved the Canadian Rockies and eventually established their homes in the western mountains, Morant at Banff and Rowed in Jasper.

The National Film Board, through the war, and over the years, has built a reputation for quality and innovation as a result of the talented film and stills photographers who worked for it. It was from their files that several Canadian postage stamps were designed based on Morant's and Rowed's wartime photographs. These were of particular interest to Nick because his father was a philatelist during his life.

Despite the similarities, Morant and Rowed did have their differences, not only of opinion, but of life styles. Rowed, for instance, loved flying, Morant hated it... Morant had a deep affection for the relaxed pace of rail travel. When it came to aerial photographs Nick claims he somehow managed to corner the job most of the time.

If the plane is going to fall apart in mid-air, I'm the man for the assignment, he would say. There was good reason for his cynicism...

Sent to join Lucien Roy of the Associated Screen News, who was representing Paramount News, to make pictures of the aerial defense network along the west coast of Vancouver Island, I arrived in Victoria, British Columbia. At the last moment, when Lucien and I were all set to go with our camera baggage assembled and ready, I received word that I would have to remain behind. The transport to be used in the air for photographs was already overloaded. They could only take one more person and they decided that Mr.Roy should go as motion pictures were far more important and immediate than stills. So Lucien went, and as he left he was kidding me: "Don't need any stills men, you guys can stay behind and drink tea!"

Away he went, and that was the last I saw of him. The following day as he was filming mock attacks and strafing runs by Canadian fighters demonstrating what the enemy would encounter should they approach Vancouver Island, his airplane was broadsided! One of the fighters came too close and they collided in mid-air; no one survived. Five people lost their lives and though Lucien's camera was found, the film was

hopelessly damaged. So it could have been that I might have been on that aircraft. Again circumstances deterred my possible demise!

The next incident occurred when we had trouble in a Bristol Bolingbroke near Mt.Mckinley in Alaska, but again Fate appeared to have been with me. It was a 'routine' assignment in 1942, a visit to Alaska where the Royal Canadian Air Force was helping to guard the continent's northern frontier from surprise attack. It was a job Harry Rowed would have loved, but of course I got stuck with it.

I was sent to make pictures of the RCAF flying in co-operation with the Americans in Alaskan defense and the defense of the Arctic. Truth of the matter was that we had an infinitesimal representation there with outdated equipment. The Americans were flying the latest Mitchell bombers and Mustang fighters while we had a few Bolingbrokes and P40s. It was difficult to glorify in photographs the efforts of the RCAF.

So Morant loaded his camera gear and went north, traveling 700 miles up the newly completed or under construction Alaska Highway, in a two-ton four-wheel drive U.S.Army truck. Covering that desolate road was also part of his assignment. He wrote back to the office saying that he was applying for a medal for war injuries sustained by mosquito attacks. *They were the size of small birds,* he claimed.

The Alaska Range, and particularly Mount McKinley, was deemed to provide an ideal background for the aerial photographs. Three P40 "Kittyhawk" fighters were to fly alongside the Bolingbroke as they were photographed. They took off first. Then, as the Bolingbroke ran up its engines in preparation for takeoff, one promptly failed. The flight was aborted and the aircrew tried to comfort Nick with the assurance that this happened often.

Even though I was in `civvies,' anytime I flew in RCAF aircraft I was often assigned extra duties besides camera work, and was essentially considered part of the crew and therefore responsible not only for doing my bit, but for the

welfare of the aircraft. There were in those days five or six crewmen, two pilots, a flight engineer, navigator and one or more air gunners and perhaps a bombardier. They flew strictly by visual reference; there were no electronic guidance systems or even radar at first, only two-way radios. Celestial navigation and dead reckoning were the only means of getting anywhere.

Half an hour later they successfully took off for their rendezvous over the mountains...

We went up in the Bolingbroke, and we were supposed to rendezvous with fighter aircraft over Mt.McKinley when I noticed something that caused my skin to crawl. I was sitting in the gunner's turret, which is on the upper part of the mid-section of the airplane. The turret affords 360 degrees of vision and, of course, the gun had been removed so that I had freedom to use my camera in all directions; it was very convenient for photography. While I was sitting there in the sunlight waiting for our rendezvous, my eyes wandered over the scenery, the cloud-scape and the aircraft. I happened to notice a line down along the wing behind the engine nacelle where there is a compartment for storage of emergency equipment, including the life raft. Wouldn't that be something, I thought, if the damn thing were to open in flight!

Some minutes later I happened to glance back to the wing and the engine nacelle where, to my horror, I saw that the compartment panel was coming off. The panel was held down by half-turn aircraft screws, but obviously something hadn't been locked tight. The panel continued to lift up in the windstorm. I hesitated reporting to the pilot since at first I couldn't believe my eyes. I thought to myself, "I'm just a civvy here and I'm on their plane and don't know anything about aircraft." I tell these guys their wing's falling off and they're going to kill themselves laughing when they get back to the mess.

All of a sudden this bloody thing ripped up and tore off - in a matter of a second it was gone. The pilot immediately called back, "What the hell happened?"

I told him, "The entire engine nacelle has

The Alaska Highway under construction in 1942. *NMC*

A Bristol Bolingbroke photographed by Morant over
Alaska in 1942, just prior to the harrowing liferaft episode on
the photo aircraft. *NMC*

Curtis P40 Kittyhawks of the Royal Canadian Air Force
fly in formation over the Alaska Range near Mt.McKinley. *NMC*

A North Atlantic convoy assembles in Halifax Harbor in the winter of 1940. *NMC*

torn off and hit the stabilizer wire on the tail fin - its broken and the radio antenna's gone too!"

Just as I was saying that, I could see the life raft starting to get air underneath it. It was a fair sized one too - a five man raft. Then the thing came loose, flew back and hit the forward part of the fin, then draped itself across one side of the tail wing. There it hung! And we started to yaw, the pilot unable to maintain course and altitude.

The pilot called back again, "What's going on now, I can't move the elevators!"

I tried to reply calmly, describing what had happened and that the life raft was now jammed across the tail-wing and elevators. I told him that I thought the only course was for him to kick the rudder hard to one side in the hopes that the air stream would carry the raft off. So he stomped on the rudder pedal and believe me, he really kicked that tail around hard, but it worked. The life raft blew off!

As quickly as it had jammed there, it was gone. I remember so distinctly seeing that thing open in the wind like a parachute, then collapse again and sail down like a piece of waste paper onto the slopes of Mt.McKinley, over which we

weren't very high. As all this was going on we had lost altitude and as we came up over one of the ridges of McKinley, all I remember is seeing the rocks getting bigger and bigger, and thinking, "By God, are we going to make it?"

The fellow below me in the belly turret admitted afterwards, "I was saying my prayers as I saw those bloody rocks going by!"

Returning to Elmendorf Air Force Base, we were a little wary since we had no radio communication after losing our antenna. We could see the anti-aircraft gunners training on us as we came over the end of the runway to land. Who's to say the Japs didn't get a Bolingbroke from somewhere and were coming in on some kind of sneak attack... or to create some sort of diversion? I was glad to get down, but the next day we went back up in another Bolingbroke and made the pictures!

Not all of Nick Morant's wartime assignments were in the air. Some involved life on the sea. Out of British Columbia, Morant was assigned to do a photo story on the Royal Canadian Navy Fisherman Reserve.

With Japan's entry into the war, and particularly the attack on Pearl Harbor, there began a hysterical fear of a west coast invasion. The resulting internment of Japanese Canadians is a sad and well known story. Military and political brass realized that the west coast of British Columbia was practically indefensible. To counteract the fear one solution was to create a naval reserve out of the west coast commercial fishing fleet. Armed only with radios, their function was to locate and identify any unusual craft, particularly Japanese submarines. They could then shadow such nefarious activities as they saw, homing in aircraft or RCN ships.

Telling this brave effort in photographs, Nick suffered three days of tortuous weather that did his stomach no good. On a larger scale, he also photographed the story of the Atlantic convoys, though, as he tells it;

The trip was far less eventful since the freighter was more stable than west coast fishing boats, and the Atlantic at the time was relatively smooth.

The ship he embarked on out of Halifax was a munitions carrier with enough explosives in the hold to send a dozen ships to the bottom of the ocean. And then there were the German U-Boats! Morant scribbled a note to his friend Colin Haworth in Montreal from an *"unidentified east coast port."* It read: *"If for any reason this damn ship should get blown sky high, will you please sorta look after things for Willie. It's unlikely, but not impossible, Thanks."* The P.S. was a full page cartoon of munitions being loaded onto a freighter with a ferocious cow looking down and saying: *"Now what the hell is HE scared about?"*

As it turned out, the trip was safe, but there was considerable reason to worry. Not far out of port, the hastily-built "Liberty" ship lost its steering and hove-to, dead in the water for two days undertaking temporary repairs while the rest of the convoy steamed on. The ship was a sitting duck for any marauding U-Boats, but fortune was with them, and they returned to the shipyards for permanent repairs. Morant got the photographs needed, pictures depicting the lifeline of ships that were absolutely necessary to maintain England and later defeat the Nazis.

A Royal Canadian Navy escort vessel on submarine patrol steams along the fringes of a convoy, hoping to curtail the German U-boat menace of World War II. *NMC*

On land, military training camps put the photographer to the test. They usually had live ammunition flying about and the job of trying to photograph young soldiers climbing through barbed wire while ducking bullets put the photographer in some equally uncomfortable and often prone positions; aiming for a picture that would tell of the risk involved for the trainees - never mind the photographer.

The Commonwealth Air Training Program offered a unique opportunity for the government to publicize the Canadian contribution to a war far from home. Morant was assigned to travel to many of the training bases constructed near small prairie towns, and again ended up taking many air to air photographs, this time often involving less experienced pilots in their training aircraft. The material Morant gathered resulted in a book that was produced outlining the outstanding training effort that produced thousands of pilots. The bases were located near towns like Brandon, Rivers, Moose Jaw, Swift Current, Medicine hat, Lethbridge, Claresholm, Fort MacLeod, DeWinton and Red Deer, to name a few. They were located in the vast open spaces away from sight, where the weather was excellent for the needs of flying training. After the war the bases often provided airports for those small towns, bringing them modern airline services.

All was not hazardous or life-threatening for photographers at the National Film Board. It was a government operation, though, and that itself held many hazards of a different kind for some men, especially a self-reliant perfectionist like Morant. He in particular insisted on processing his own negatives and prints, while on assignment. That meant hauling along not only cameras and lighting equipment, but also a travelling laboratory in special trunks so that he could develop and print photographs almost anywhere. But he had to rely on the Film Board office to ship supplies as needed. It was not unusual for the office to receive a testy cable from Morant. One read: WHEN YOU LOCATE THOSE SUPPLIES YOU CLAIM TO HAVE SENT TO ME PLEASE RUSH THEM. I NEED TO FINISH THIS ASSIGNMENT BEFORE MY RETIREMENT.

A North American AT-6 Texan trainer, known as a Harvard in the Royal Canadian Air Force, overflies a training base in southern Manitoba. The Harvard was an advanced trainer and thousands were built in Canada by various companies such as Noordyn in Montreal and Canadian Car in Winnipeg. *NMC*

A DeHaviland Chipmunk basic trainer, flies over its aerodrome somewhere in southern Alberta. The landing strip is a large circular grass pasture, there are no paved runways at this Commonwealth Air Training base. *NMC*

Above: An RCAF trainee and his instructor discuss an impending flight on a hot summer day somewhere on Canada's prairies during the war years. This photograph was an inspiration for a Canadian 7 cent stamp. The inset photograph shows the stamp on a background photo that Morant made, with two airmen and a civilian gentleman showing them the proper directions on their map! That gentleman is Morant himself. *NMC*

Opposite page: A flight of RCAF Harvards formate over Abbotsford, B.C. on an intensive training flight. Two thousand two hundred fifty eight Harvards were purchased by the RCAF, only one other aircraft, the Avro Anson was purchased in greater numbers. *NMC*

Opposite page: With Mt.Baker looming in the background, Harvards of the Commonwealth Air Training Program fly past the Abbotsford control tower before breaking for their landing. *NMC*

Above: A Harvard taxis past the flight line on a training mission at an airbase somewhere in Canada during World War II. *NMC*

At Dorval, in Montreal, aircraft of various markings are staged for ferry flights across the Atlantic to England. Canadian Pacific organized its Ferry Command department in 1940 to deliver aircraft overseas and trained bush and airline pilots to crew the aircraft. In the photograph at left, a Lockheed Ventura taxis past two Hudsons, one of which has just started its port engine. Behind them are B-24s and Venturas in USAAF markings and the twin tail of a B-25 Mitchell. In the foreground is an RAF B-24 Liberator.

The photograph at right is a photo montage that Morant manipulated in his darkroom. It shows the flight line of the RAF Ferry Command at Dorval and beating up the airfield is a B-25 Mitchell and a Lockheed Hudson. *NMC*

In another montage, Morant put together this
photograph depicting anti-submarine defenses on the east
coast. Flying overhead the Fairmyle anti-submarine patrol
boats is a Hudson bomber painted in Coastal Defense
Command's two tone grey camouflage. *NMC*

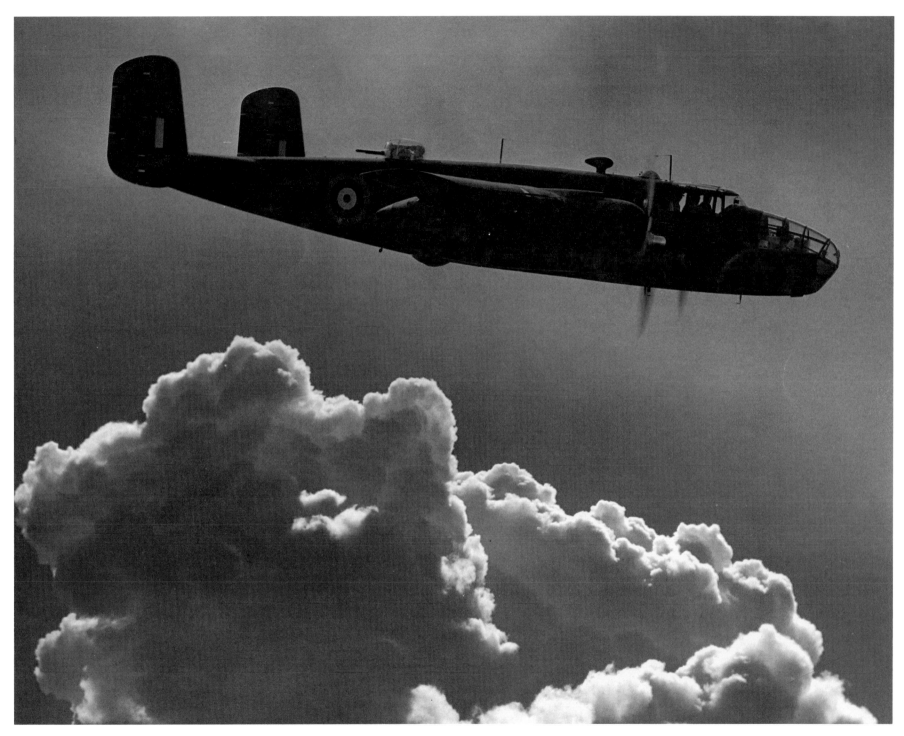

A North American B-25 Mitchell bomber, beginning its
long ferry flight to England in 1942 is nicely silhouetted by
Morant from a photo plane. *NMC*

Opposite page: Because of wartime camouflage, it is impossible to make out the name of this ocean liner preparing to depart Halifax Harbor with a load of troops in the winter of 1942. It appears to be one of Canadian Pacific's Atlantic service Empresses, and that is likely why Morant made this shot of the vessel. *NMC*

The photograph at left shows workmen positioning an eight-ton cast iron replacement propellor for a Yugoslav merchantman in drydock at Halifax receiving wartime repairs. In background is a line of Corvettes preparing for the next Atlantic convoy to depart. *NMC*

The photo above, composed and orchestrated by
Morant, became the 50 cent Canadian stamp shown in the
inset. *NMC*

His persistence in developing and printing his own work was no reflection on the staff in Ottawa. They were highly professional. One of them, Louis Jaques, brother of Ronny, and a news photographer in his own right, was highly thought of by Nick as one of the best darkroom men in the country. *He could get more out of a negative than anyone else,* claimed Nick.

This intensity about his work may have been what made those occasional flashes of horse-play for which Morant was noted, a necessity. Without the release provided by some utter nonsense now and then, the strain of personal perfection could have risked his health. He has always had a preoccupation with health that is balanced only by a strange sense of humor.

On one occasion, C.D.Howe, Canada's indefatigable Minister of National Defence, announced an unveiling ceremony for the first artillery piece to be produced in the country. The managers of the factory were impressed, particularly since they had just received the blueprints and an example of the artillery piece only a few months before, and were not yet in production. They had to hurriedly reassemble the gun, as it had been dismantled in order to duplicate the parts, for the public unveiling in front of all the political and military brass, as well as the press. Morant was there to record this bit of history, but like all the press in Ottawa, he knew the story behind this modern miracle of war production.

The fake Canadian artillery piece may have limited some of the respect Morant might have had for the accomplishment as the Minister and his cronies clustered around the weapon. As the press cameras flashed, a deep voice with an imitation-Russian accent whispered loudly: *Not yat, Boris. Da fuse eesn'y lit...*

Fortunately only a few people in the press section could hear the remark. There were snickers enough to ruin some exposures: an RCMP officer twitched, but maintained his composure.

Morant went through the war using his atrocious accent. Sometimes he signed letters; Count Alexis Boris Torispantzoff, an old vaudeville name. One evening, hanging out of the window of a Halifax hotel, completely sober by the way, he harangued anyone who would listen of the great days ahead, *cawms de rewolution.* He missed arrest and internment principally because his accent was so patently fraudulent.

The biggest event of World War II, if one excepts the atomic bomb, was the Founding of the United Nations in San Francisco in April, 1945. Hitler was hiding in Berlin and the Americans were about to invade Japan. Morant was assigned to record Canada's participation in this historic conference. Two thousand of the world's best newsmen were there along with dignitaries from all the Allied nations and third world countries.

A few months prior to being sent to the San Francisco conference, Nick developed complications from surgery he had had as a result of continuing complications from the grizzly bear accident. He had sent in for an expense advance prior to travelling to California, but got a message back saying that the advance would not be sent because the Accounting Department had not received his previous month's statement. He replied: RETELL EXPENSE TURNDOWN PLEASE RUSH MAGIC CARPET OR THREE HUNDRED TO CONTINUE WORK STOP SINCE WHEN DO I HAVE TO FINANCE A GOVERNMENT JOB TO SATISFY A BUNCH OF BUGEYED ACCOUNTANTS STOP IF THERE IS NO MONEY THEN NO FURTHER KODAK STOP TELL THAT TO DEAR OLD BIRDLEGS AND REMEMBER I LOVE YOU

MORANT

Needless to say Nick never quite grasped the complications of an accountant's life in government departments charged with spending public money. It was poetic when he filed one expense account answering the query "Purpose of Travel" with the response:

"Pure unadulterated pleasure." Somehow the account went through!

Expense accounts seemed to get Morant into varying degrees of trouble, but only once did matters take on a serious note. He had been talking casually to a close friend, a newsman, about some government cheques he had received, some for salary, some for expenses, none of which he felt entitled to. It made for an interesting newspaper item entitled "Generous Ottawa."

Though the article did not mention Nick by name, the writer, tongue in cheek, accused the federal Treasury Department of putting temptations in the way of honest employees. Newspapers all over Canada reprinted the item.

Enter the RCMP!

A menacing detective from the Force turned up in the writer's office demanding the name of the "innocent fellow" (there appeared to be doubt in his voice about such innocence and some mention of possible retribution for illegal actions). The ensuing controversy involved everyone on the staff of the publication right up to the president and senior editor, but the consensus was that sources had to be protected.

But Morant said he had nothing to hide, a talk with police and a Crown Prosecutor cleared his name. The offence seemed trivial to Nick until the Mounties told him they had just broken the operation of a payroll man in one government department. The man would send out unauthorized cheques to individuals, wait to see if they were cashed, and if so, would show up at the individual's home explaining he had made an error and was in fear of losing his job. After a few friendly visits, and more cheques, he would say that things seemed safe for him to continue if the proceeds could be split. It took good character evaluation to find those who would succumb, but he seemed able to line quite a few up, reaping a fair amount of taxable income in the process. If the fake cheques were returned, the potential conspirator

In support of the war effort, Morant made this photograph of Noordyn Norseman light utility aircraft for the Royal Canadian Air Force in final assembly at the Montreal plant. One hundred of these aircraft were built for the RCAF during 1940, subsequently rendered surplus in 1957 and sold, some still soldiering on as bush aircraft in northern Ontario today. *NMC*

A steel foundary at Hamilton, Ontario, circa 1945. *NMC*

units that fired off flash bulbs. Often assistants would hold the flash unit at an advantageous angle away from the subject, tethered to the camera by a 30-foot umbilical cord.

One American photographer who had rushed down there along with Morant, was having difficulty making his shot, and had no one to hold his flash. So he turned to a man standing near him who was just watching and said: "Hey Mac. Grab this and hold it up just like this. No! Go that way! That's it. Good. Just keep it there. Don't move now. All right gentlemen!" Flash - he made his shot.

The gentleman holding the flash was none other than Lord Halifax! The American photographer was totally oblivious as to who he was!

By late 1945 the war propaganda job was losing its excitement. Italy and Austria surrendered on May 2; Hitler obliterated Eva and himself in a Berlin bunker, Germany surrendered unconditionally within five days. The first atomic bomb was dropped on Japan on August 6, Japan surrendered by September 1. Morant worked in three hectic weeks of Western Canada assignments after the San Francisco conference, then pausing in Banff, began to get the brush-off from Ottawa when he sent in suggestions for further stories. For seven weeks he sat idle, with not a reply from Ottawa. Had the National Film Board been disbanded?

Ralph Foster, head of the Graphics Division, returned from a trip to London only to find a new appointee in his office. It seemed that now was the time for Morant to return to the CPR. He had been the first photographer taken on to start the Film Board's still photo department and felt reasonably satisfied with his part in the war. He arranged for the "loan" of his services to be revoked - he was back in the employ of the railway for the third time in his career.

A covered bridge in eastern Canada. *NMC*

Part III

The Prime Years

The Singing Gypsy

A book of poems by Mollie Morant, photos by Nicholas Morant

The Singing Gypsy

Straight from his heart his song
Of joy or sorrow,
Tears of today,
Sunshine tomorrow.
Just as his heart tells,
So sing the birds -
Music that stirs the soul,
Songs without words.
Not down the dark ways
Of thoughts goes he,
Life he knows as a bird
Knows land and sea.

Down the green Roman road
In the grey gloaming
I heard his haunting voice
As he went roaming;
Now when the dawn breaks
All will be still
Where the old road goes
Under the hill.

Church Of St. Francis

. . . St. Francis speaks.

"Turn in and rest -
So few come now to pray;
The squirrel comes here,
And the insolent jay
Flirts his blue wings
All the long summer day.

Sometimes a deer comes,
Stepping o'er the dead
On pointed feet,
With lifted, antlered head -
And noiseless owls
When all the west is red.

And when my door
Stands open to the sun
I kneel and watch
The velvet field mice run.
And in the Autumn spined porcupine
Crosses the path, toward the fallen vine.
Will you not rest? I do not bid you pray."

. . . I hid my face, the vision passed away.

The Goose Woman

Why should she fear
What the future brings,
When fat are the bodies
And sleek are the wings

Of geese for market,
With hives of bees,
And the cow lowing
Under the trees,

And God in an Ikon
Close on her wall
To answer her prayers
Should ill befall?

Steel Bird

When Adam was from Eden cast
To mourn through time for Eve's misdeed,
Cheating the Angels' watchful eyes
He brought away the Poppy's seed
To give him dreams to meet his need,
The blest, accursed Poppy seed.

Perhaps in such a sleep he dreamed
Of men with wings, not angel hosts,
And ships that raced with snowy wings
And horses going by like ghosts;
So swift they seemed, the lovely things,
Fleeing at dawn as if with wings.

But Adam's nobler sons today
Have put away the drowsy flower;
High o'er the clouds they take their way,
Serene and swift in splendid power,
Through sunlit heights, o'er storm and shower,
Having his dreams for all their dower.

Request

Blue scabious now along the Downs are flowering,
And harebells and sweet thyme to scent the air
Strong from the sea-weeds left by clean tides ebbing -
Would I were there!

Would I were there, a spirit disembodied,
To climb lightfoot those chalky paths again:
Freed from this grief of living and remembering,
From love and pain.

O gentle Death, when you draw close beside me
Let me see clear those hills I love and know,
And let the falling dusk of your oblivion
Like English twilight grow.

Fish Boats

When I was young
The home I knew
Was roofed in moss
That shone with dew.

I woke to hear -
Sweet sound to me -
The fishing boats
Put out sea

In dripping mists
That veiled the sky
Where in the dawn
The duck went by.

In storm or quiet
Sunset light,
Home with the gulls
They came ere night.

The Lombardys

My father's father
Planted these trees -
Slim green wands
That bent to the breeze

Year by year
he watched them grow,
Till his hour
Came to go.

Then my father
Sought their shade,
Leaning to sharpen
His scythe's long blade.

Now I, for a season,
Shall hear each Spring
High in their branches
The first larks sing.

Totem Poles

At Ankor and on Easter Isle,
At Athens and in Rome,
Stand temples to forgotten Gods,
To Gods who came not home
Some evening when their worshippers
Brought gift of blood or wine
To pour on vacant altars
Within an echoing shrine.

Now here, where all the years drift by
Marked but by storm and tide,
And all the ancient life is gone
And only as you abide,
I stand before you, frowning ones,
And know you, too, must fall
And all your cult and grandeur
Be gone beyond recall.
I like to think that otherwhere
The old Gods gather yet
To keep a tryst with Destiny
Tho' mortal men forget.

Waiting

O Rocket, of your sweetness give:
Ring, Columbine, your purple bell.
The blackbirds and the thrushes sing,
"The Spring has come, and all is well."

Above the moors the curlews call,
The wind comes fragrant from the sea,
And bells of hidden churches plead
For faiths that were and yet may be.

O Rocket, of you sweetness give:
I would forget the lives men mar,
And hear you in my garden wait
The beauty of the evening star.

Old Smith

He Has returned to earth again
Who scarcely left the earth for long,
For he was deaf to Beauty's voice
And found no joy in book or song.

Say then that green things grew for him
Who bent o'er them with eyes grown dim.

He has returned to earth and lies
Content at last, all tasks fulfilled,
While still his team moves orderly
Across the acres that he tilled.

He will not miss the bird's spring song
To whom spring meant the days grew long.

Iron Letters

Under a leaden sky the road winds on
Between bare hedgerows, where west wind sings,
Beyond the sedgy fields a white capped sea -
Grey as gull's wings.

The hunt has passed, the cattle stand at gaze
Watching the scarlet coats move far away -
I hear a horn deep in an unseen wood,
Sad as an echo in the dusk of day.

Over my head the plover, wheeling, come
To light again in flocks, where men rode by,
And solitude steals back to claim her own
The wide wet fields, the vast and vacant sky.

Foothill Sunset

Once under flaring sunsets such as this
On these same sand dunes Indians laid their dead.
Who knows if, even as I today, they heard
The mourning doves o'erhead
In these old pine trees? Long ere white men came
They crossed this valley, silent in the heat
Their gaunt hounds following, noiseless in the dust
Of unshod ponies' feet.

Now where the barbed wire stretches - acres wide,
And slowly through the fields piped waters flow,
there stands the Chinaman from dawn to dark,
In ancient patience, leaning on his hoe.

Prophecy

Massed elms above the cornfields stand today
Casting their shade where the loud reapers go.
I see them while I stare across these hills
At the mountains crowned with snow.

There where the lane winds on in sun and shade
The Gypsies with their painted wagons pass,
Seeking the Roman's way with trees and pools
To camp among the grass.

Waking, yet in a dream, I ride again
And see their faces, brown hands on my rein,
And hear a voice foretell this grief for me:
"You shall cross seas, and not come back again."

Vision

Where silver birches leaning
Made shadow on the stream
I saw a knight ride through the ford,
    I saw his armour gleam -
    And water splashed like diamonds against the low sun's
        beam.

The gay green of the beeches
Threw up like painted things
The crimson on his bridle rein,
The gold and silver rings -
The rings of mail that heathens wrought to guard the
breasts of kings.

And ere the woodland took him
And he turned and looked behind,
And the beauty of his quiet face
    It sank into my mind -
    The beauty born of chivalry that only dreamers find.

Monument To Failure

Sunlight and peace -
That peace man conquered leaves -
Gaunt ruin and blown dust
Where once were home and sheaves.

These are their monuments
Where none will kneel -
The homely, long-dried pump
And broken wheel.

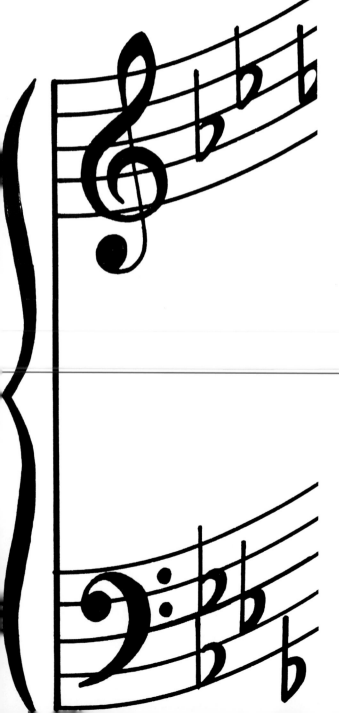

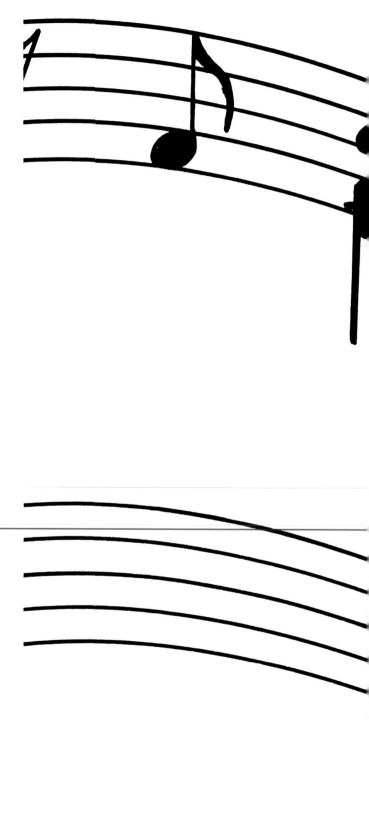

Morant continues...

Next my thoughts turned to a visual presentation coupled with musical accompaniment. Over the years I built up a collection of pictures that made me think of certain pieces of music, and vice-versa, certain pieces of music reminded me of photographs I had made. I organized the photos based on the musical pieces and found that the end result was a series of themes.Certain bars of music suggested certain scenes and the photographs were matched to appear as that particular bar of music was played. In the presentation of the photographs, it was necessary to wait for a certain bar of music before bringing the photograph on, in order to gain the full impact of the visual impression, backed by the sound.

What we did in the end was to put together a number of those groups of photographs with accompanying music to produce a show an hour and half long. One of the themes we called "The World At Your Feet." Another was "Skyscapes," and one was on Arizona, which I had wanted to put to the "Grand Canyon Suite," but there was no way I could do it to my satisfaction! In still pictures it is very difficult to show movement, such as lightning. No matter how hard I tried, I was dissatisfied with any effect I attempted.

There is an interesting aside to this problem. The gentleman living next door at that time was a biological advisor to the Walt Disney company. Many Disney wildlife films were being produced around Banff in those days, and my neighbor was employed for the purpose of ensuring the accuracy of species names and habitats.

He came over one day when I was involved in one of my frustrating rehearsals. I was not getting anywhere. In rehearsal you are more careless, constantly trying different things, and when you make a mistake, you start all over again. In front of an audience you are more careful and have a set program you stick with, but when you make a mistake, you just do your best to cover it up and carry on with the show.

When my neighbor arrived, I turned off the projector and we had tea. "What were you doing down there in the dark?" he enquired. Willie and I hadn't been able to achieve anything, but I

The CANADIAN ROCKIES in NATURAL COLOUR

"A TALK WITHOUT WORDS"

presented by

NICHOLAS MORANT

173

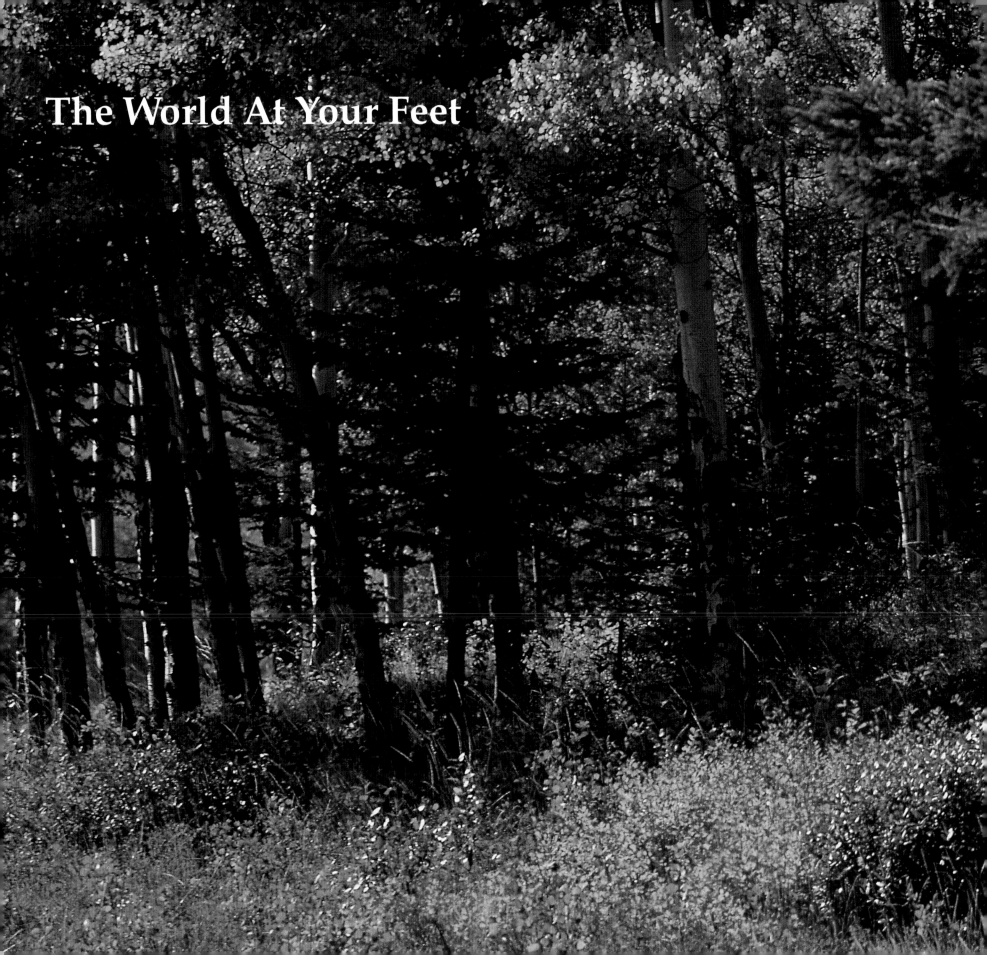

The World At Your Feet

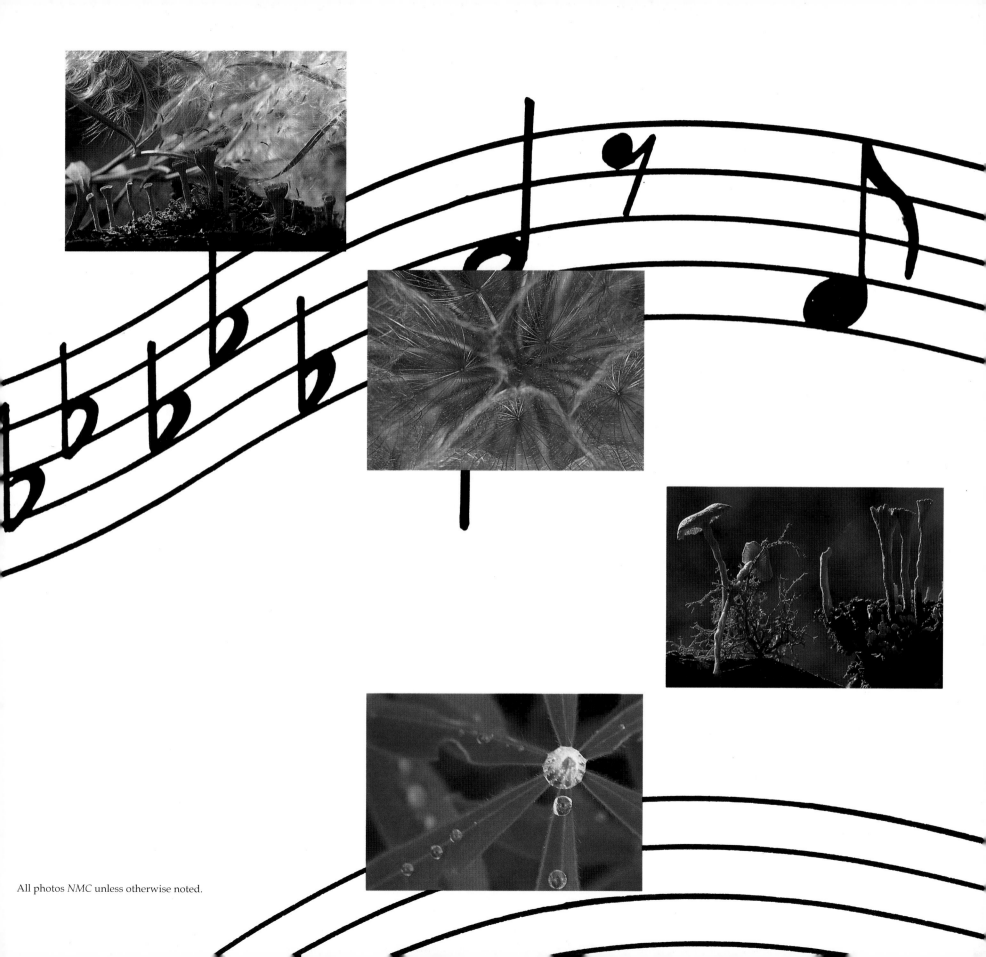

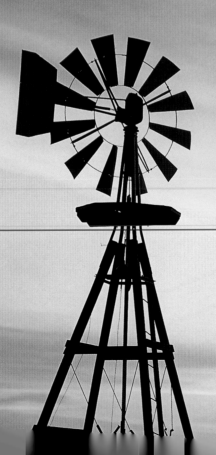

Skyscapes

told him I was trying to do the "Grand Canyon Suite" in still photographs. I mentioned that I thought it was impossible to match the score with the photographs I had. "If you want to," I told him, "I'll show you what the problem is."

So I turned the projector back on and picked up where I had left off. Passing through a number of scenes, I turned and said to him, "The trouble is that it needs to be presented in motion pictures, not stills. There's no life, no movement!"

"I think you're right," he remarked, "there might be a possibility here!"

Two years later Disney presented the "Grand Canyon Suite" with a huge orchestra and some beautiful motion picture footage. To this day I don't know whether it was produced just by coincidence or not, since my neighbor passed away shortly after his visit, before the film was released.

Getting back to the subject, however, Willie and I eventually put together presentations that we felt confident with, and for fifteen years we presented the show in front of audiences, big and small, throughout North America. On average we did one show a month over those years, in between fulfilling the needs of company assignments as per usual.

The show took some twelve years to put together and it was indeed my idea, not the CPR's. I did need their acceptance to do the shows in conjunction with my other responsibilities and, of course I would, in the introduction to the show, explain that I was in fact employed by the Canadian Pacific Railway.

When the Morant's finally got their show put together, they started doing it voluntarily in Boy Scout halls and church basements. Then they went into the Canadian Pacific Hotels, but were not treated as celebrities as Nick was just another CPR employee. He and Willie had to organize everything themselves; they were on the list as an overhead -an expense, so it was difficult to enlist help from the hotel staff...

And if you were there week after week throughout the summer, staff support became almost non-existant, claimed Nick. Before every show, different fellows would set up the seating and they would put all the seats, some two or three hundred of them, in a line, rather than offset so that people could see the screen. One of the things Willie and I did was to shift all those chairs so that they were offset. You couldn't expect people to set things up the way you wanted them, so we generally preferred to do it ourselves.

Out of necessity, I began providing all my own equipment. I would go into an auditorium at three in the afternoon, and it would take me at least two hours to make sure that things were arranged, tables set up, equipment checked and everything ready. Willie made velvet coverlets and decorative mats that served a two-fold purpose: to protect the equipment in transit and to provide theatrical colour. She lined those covers with gold brocade and used the most expensive velvet. When people arrived the projector was set up and covered with one of the scarlet pieces of velvet, and the loudspeakers had little covers on them. Willie was the key to my giving such a show: she was indispensable and backed me up in so many hidden ways.

Everything was done in good taste; there was none of this business of fiddling around getting a book to prop up the projector, or having images dancing around the screen every time you changed slides. She made sure all the preliminary arrangements were taken care of prior to the show, not ten minutes before. And then she quietly 'orchestrated' the performance from the back of the room while I fed the slides into the Leica projector by hand, silently, and effected the dissolve with a silk-gloved hand. We tried to provide a little showmanship and professionalism, as well as a good show.

Prior to show time, ten or fifteen minutes early, I'd come into the auditorium. Willie would busy herself with the tape recorders (there would be two tape recorders in case one failed, as well as two PA systems - we had a backup for everything) making sure everything was ready to go. I would be dressed in a dinner jacket; Willie in a nice evening outfit, surrounded by the colour of those dust covers that looked so attractive.

I would wander around and talk to the people who had arrived. "Good evening. Where are you from?" I'd ask.

"Oh, we're from St.Louis, Missouri." If I knew something about the place I'd say, "Ah, the home of the Missouri Times Daily, isn't it?"

"Yes, have you read our paper?", they'd ask.

After fifteen minutes I had talked to a good half of the audience seated. By then I'd already won over a good portion of the people, even before I had started. Then I would start the show off with about ten minutes of images backed by a running commentary. "You all may have come here this evening because of this picture, but we'd like to show you the behind-the-scenes view of how we were able to make it." Then I'd go on and explain why we were doing the show, that it was all a... "grand plot by the Canadian Pacific Railway and the Government of Canada to get tourists up here to spend their money."

The thing was that for ten minutes they heard a little about the CPR and I would mention that many people might not realize it, but Canadian Pacific isn't just a railway, giving them some facts and figures on what else they were involved in. Most of the Americans didn't realize this. For instance, I would tell them that Western Union doesn't exist here, that the two railways operate their own system under their own names but are able to feed into Western Union.

Then I had a light dimmer, controlled by a rheostat beside my signal box, by which I could bring up an amber light on the screen. The house lights were long out, and in the darkness I would bring up the amber light, then walk up in front where I would be in silhouette, just a figure outlined on the screen. I would then say, "You now know who I am and how I earn my living. I want you now to use your imagination and think of an art gallery. This art gallery has a series of rooms, each of which is full of pictures related to certain subjects. In another room is an orchestra, maybe in rehearsal, playing music that just by chance enhances the mood of the pictures you are seeing. When you go to an art gallery, you look at the pictures and accept or reject them for what they are; you don't need anyone telling you what colour of paint was used or what kind of paper. All you're interested in is the title and the result, so this is the little game we'll play." With that, the show would commence.

I still have all the original slides for our "Talk Without Words," but I have long since forgotten the music and the sequence. We would come in with the first piece, I believe it was called "Gymnopedie," a lively piece that portrayed quiet places. Then we followed with a speedier one, and I would ask the audience if they had ever been to Nova Scotia or the New England states? They have a host of remarkable things on the tops of their barns - weather vanes! I had fourteen shots accompanied by some very fast music and it was all I could do to keep up with it and end at the right time. It ended on a very high note, so you had to have the last slide into the projector on time or you would miss the finale. I don't know how many times I rehearsed that!

I never wrote anything down. When I got through to a certain point in the show, I knew how much more I had to go. I would know that I had seven more slides to present, but it was often by guess that I got the last one in on time. Sometimes I used to pull dirties and give myself an extra slide in case I fluffed it - nobody would ever know the difference!

At the end of one section I would again turn up my amber light, walk up and say; "How many of you have been for a walk in the countryside and perhaps been aware that you are crushing something beautiful under your feet!" Then back to the projector, drop my amber down, and I'd bring up my first slide. You would see images of mosses and lichens and flowers and insects with the sounds of some selected symphonies. I didn't know the names of half the things I photographed, certainly not their proper names anyway, but that wasn't the exercise. Each of the different subjects would be organized in three-minute groupings, the entire show would run with little commentary for the next hour and a half. And that was it.

We did that show for something like fifteen years in all manner of places - even in a mental institution. Mostly, we had audiences who were most appreciative, ranging from 35 people to 3,600 people at the Peabody auditorium in Daytona Beach, Florida. We would do 14 or 15 lectures a year in Canada and the USA; the CPR discovered slowly that these lectures didn't harm their image at all; that it didn't cost them much more than what I was already paid, and they hoped to make a few friends along the way. This was what is known as an institutional advertisement.

If there was someone in the audience who came up and talked to me after a show who would have some comment about the Company that I thought was worth passing on, I would forward it to the head of whatever department was appropriate. I once ran into two ladies in Victoria who came up and complimented me on the show, but said it was not so nice knowing that the CPR was polluting their water. I asked them where they lived, and they replied, "Up Island near a place called Crofton."

There was a logging railway up there and it was ours. We were spraying insecticide along the right-of-way and it was seeping into the wells. I thought, "My God, these people have a problem and they obviously weren't getting any response from anyone."

So I turned that one over to one of our Vice-Presidents in Montreal and a stop was immediately put to that practice. Montreal had been aware of complaints, but they had not been approached firsthand, so they sent someone responsible out to see about the matter, and things were remedied.

One story I want to tell you occurred at the Banff Springs Hotel and the Chateau Lake Louise. During our summer for a number of years we would present our show on Sunday nights, since that was an open night when other performances weren't going on, and we'd alternate hotels.

I always enjoyed putting the show on at the Banff Springs as we had good audiences, and you never knew who would be out there. I remember an old gentleman who got up in the middle of one show and walked up the front aisle in the middle of the picture, and as he walked by he apologized in a whisper that could be heard all over Mount Stephen Hall. He said, "Awful sorry to have to leave early, but I have weak kidneys!"

The gentleman was hard of hearing, and what to him was a whisper was to us a rather loud voice. Of course, everyone heard this and there was much laughter.

There was one occasion that I well remember, one that pleased me very much. I was at the Chateau Lake Louise and in the room we used there were sofas as well as chairs to sit on. People used to rush for those sofas because they were very comfortable, and you could sit and watch the show for an hour and a half without getting numb. Anyway, there were two couples sitting on this one big sofa, and they were influential American businessmen. The ladies were exquisitely clad; Willie had already drawn my attention to them when she said, "There's some money over there!"

The gentlemen were wearing white cravats and vests, white coats and sported great cigars. When I saw them, they were all sitting back waiting for the entertainment to begin as if they'd seen it all before.

I went down and said hello to them and found out they were from Los Angeles. We talked about a few things, and as I was about to continue on my rounds, one of the men said to me, "Are you going to talk about this accident you had with a bear?"

I replied, "It's not a pleasant story. One man is dead, his wife committed suicide, and much of the rest is best left untold."

The man countered, "We understood that there would be a story about the bear!"

"Well," I said, "I just don't want to go on about it; you should be able to understand, I'd nearly seen the end myself; surely you can understand that!"

"We'd heard that you had this bear story," the fellow insisted.

So I did the show and they watched through it. When it was over, they came up and said it was a good show and left.

A week later, in Banff, the same four people were there. I talked with them and said, "Game for more punishment?"

"We enjoyed it very much the last time,"

they replied.

I said, "I thought maybe you were so disappointed at the lack of action without the bear story that you'd have gotten up and left in the middle of the show. I hope you understand that this is exactly the same show you saw last week with the exception of a few minor changes. When it took twelve years to put together, there's not likely to be another one! And there's no bear story in it."

I did the show again. When it was over, they got up and came over to me at the projector.

"Mr. Morant, we want to tell you, you've made us remember things that we'd long forgotten. We had forgotten that many of the things you showed us even exist!"

They both gave me their cards; President of the *Los Angeles Times,* and General sales Manager for Advertising for the other Los Angeles paper, both of which were Hearst newspapers. When you get tough nuts like that, you've done well to gain their compliments. They were very disappointed not to hear the bear story, but I had some reprints made of the story that was in the *Saturday Post* and sent them each a copy.

In Nick's day, modern computer controlled slide dissolve units were not available, nor would he have used them if they were:

They were too noisy! One of the things Willie and I had was a signalling system that I built, strung between us. During the show she was never beside me, always in another part of the room, back or side. She had to know, and I had to know, first, if she was ready to go and, second, when. So we developed a signal system between us, rather than my saying, "Are you ready?" Or having one of those noise makers that go `click-clack,' next slide please! And the projectionist would put the slide in upside down...

That reminds me of a story about Dan McCowan, one of my friends who was an author and fellow resident of Banff. He used to lecture, and I actually followed him in the circuit sometimes. But Danny once had in his audience a man by the name of Carveth Wells, who was

himself a famous lecturer in the United States. He was the dean of American lecturers, well respected and liked, and it was an honour to have him in the audience.

He came up to see Danny afterwards and complimented his show. "I really liked your show, but you know,' he said, `you really let me down, Danny!"

"What do you mean?" asked McCowan.

"Well," he said, "I don't know, I always put a slide in upside down so that my show isn't always so perfect! The audience just loves to get something on me!"

All lecturers, I imagine, have little tricks that they use and they are usually developed from years of experience. A lot of them work very well.

Dan McCowan, Banff naturalist, and friend of the Morant's, overlooking the Bow River with Mount Howard Douglas in the background. *NMC*

On the roof of the "Canadian" as it negotiates the curves of the Crowsnest Subdivision, Gene Wilder's stand-in (at right) fights off the bad guy in the movie "Silver Streak." The photograph below shows the camera crew packing up their gear after a successful shoot as the train stands at the east switch of Crowsnest yard, November 1975. *NMC*

CHAPTER TEN
The CPR and Motion Pictures

One of the biggest responsibilities of Nick Morant's position with the CPR as 'Special Photographer' for Public Relations was the co-ordination and collaboration between motion picture companies and the railway. The most notable films he was involved with were "Silver Streak," "Superman II" and "Days of Heaven" (originally titled "Gates of Heaven"). Projects other than Hollywood extravaganzas included the made-for-television series "The National Dream," based on the book by Pierre Berton, and numerous other Canadian Pacific advertising and promotional films. Great amounts of money were involved in the Hollywood productions particularly, and the CPR stood to gain revenue payments for use of equipment and facilities. Therefore, it was in the best interests of the Company to make someone available to the movie producers, someone who not only had a knowledge of the motion picture business, but knew railroading and the matter of safety...

My prime responsibility when the CPR became involved with the movie business - my instructions from the top brass - was to make sure that the motion picture people who paid their way got their money's worth. This involved quite an overwhelming responsibility because, for one thing, the contract would read, and I quote, "Time will be of the essence, always." And so, if you were on a set and you had a train facing the wrong direction, for instance, then the CPR was at fault and we were now liable for the time that they lost while we turned the train around.

I very quickly worked out a plan that I used forever when I was doing work with movie people. The local division Assistant Superintendent was usually the man in charge of the railroad personnel assigned to run trains or prepare the property for the filming. I had nothing to do with that. I was there in case there

was an argument. If the Assistant Superintendent felt something was not safe, or if they weren't able to fulfil the movie company's requests, I would act as judge to see if the Assistant Superintendent was correct in his actions. If it was a matter of safety, I usually backed the CPR official; however, if there was any question about the matter, I had a 'hot-line' to Montreal and my contact then was Mr.Stinson, later President of the railway, and he was a great help to me.

I came to know something of the movie business through efforts I made to produce and photograph films back in the 30's, whilst I still worked for the <u>Winnipeg Free Press.</u> I met a fellow named Dennison Thornton, who wrote for an art magazine in Winnipeg, a sort of answer to Saturday Night, in the midwest. He used to write theater and movie criticisms, and he was interested in motion pictures as art. He was involved in one of the first documentary film clubs formed in Canada, and he persuaded me to join. We used to rent a theater on Sunday nights to show some of the films we'd rent, or that someone had produced locally. a lot of them were very left-wing pro-communist propaganda films, but they were free.

Denny Thornton wanted to make a movie; he wanted to direct it and because I was the only one he knew with a movie camera, I was chosen as the photographer! I had had a chance to purchase a 35mm movie camera, a French-made 'DeBrie,' while with the <u>Free Press.</u> The big problem was that our amassed bank accounts could only provide enough film for one minute of shooting, and then we'd have to wait a month or so to do the next scene. It was an impossible situation, but believe me, we tried.

Normally, a film is shot randomly. That is to say, when you were in one location, you shot everything you could, then moved on to the next location, not worrying about where in the film each sequence belonged. It was for the editor to cut everything and splice the film in its proper

sequence and order. Alas, we didn't have an editor. We had to film what we wanted in its proper sequence, so we figured we might as well start at the beginning and get a good opening as we might never be able to afford the rest of the film.

It was a thing that was doomed to failure from the start, but we spent thousands of hours in Child's Restaurant over cups of coffee, discussing camera angles and techniques. I remember Thornton having a really good idea, an idea that today would be considered trite. We would open the picture with a bottle of milk. We then pan up the bottle of milk, which was frozen, the cap pushed up, typical of Winnipeg. Then the camera would pan up to a hand grasping the bottle, to the man looking at his bottles. That was the first shot. What the last one was I don't know; I doubt we ever got that far!

Joe Pechette was one of the guys involved in the documentary film club and he was good fun, because he wanted to make money at it - he was a good Jewish boy and proud of it! He didn't think too much of Gentiles; they had no zip. So Pechette would go out and sell somebody on what in those days was called a 'trailer.' I don't know what they are called today; I don't even think they exist in the industry anymore.

A trailer was a two or three-minute commercial made for the screen of a local neighborhood theater, and if you sold it to the right people, it might get into five or six theaters. So we would go after a client such as <u>Winnipeg Supply and Fuel Company,</u> which was very big in those days, and was quite a heavy advertiser. The ads were something like 'Brick Warehouse' ads except they weren't in colour. We would put a little music in the background; that was the best we could do, but we did have printed titles! They were the same thing as today's commercials that you see on television except that they didn't have the pizzazz that they do now. They were simply photographed - horrible too, I might add.

Great times were had at Child's Restaurant in Winnipeg (all the movie 'elite' hung out at Child's), they gave everyone a second cup of coffee free, even if that's all you bought. Not many restaurants, then or today, are that liberal with their customers. The late night shift was supervised by a fellow whose name was Nick. He later opened up a restaurant of his own down the street where Morant would regularly go for supper. It was known as 'Nick's Place' and though Morant didn't realize it at the time, the owner capitalized on his patronage - he told everyone that the Free Press photographer ate there...!

I remember discussing with Pechette, again at Child's, how we would sell these trailers. Joe would go out and propose a deal to Winnipeg Supply; "I've got a great deal for you," he'd say. "I can give you six theaters, matinees, shown twice a day, once during the day and once in the evening."

Many of the theaters had an organist or musicians playing, sometimes a whole orchestra, before the show started. The Capital was a Famous Players theater, and in each city they had a local band called the 'Capitolians.' The most famous one seemed to be in Winnipeg - Earl Hill and his 'Capitolians.' They had an orchestra pit with a pneumatic floor that rose up as the music played. They would play some numbers and then there would be a novelty cartoon with the bouncing ball that you sang along with; and that was the sort of era it was...

Pechette would be sitting in Child's and he'd be berating us Gentiles. "I don't understand how you guys can even exist," he'd say. "How you eat I don't know, you're so dumb!"

I had just asked the question of the day: "Joe, where are you going to get the money for film in the first place because I don't have any!"

"It'll be there," he'd say, "you'll see."

Then it suddenly dawned on me that I had taken on a project that would shake the timbers of 20th Century, all for a hundred dollars! The film alone cost one hundred twenty -five!

So I said to Joe, "All right, now how do you

work this?"

"Well, you go make the pictures. In the meantime I'm out selling. I sold Winnipeg Supply, now I've got to go out and get a theater. I'll go down and see Benny at the Capital."

"Benny," he says, "you're a good friend of mine, you've been like an uncle to me. I'm like a nephew to you; we're almost blood brothers. Benny, I want you should show my pictures, my trailers, in your theater!"

And Benny replies; "That, that, I'm putting that on in my theater here! I've got good people here. I can't be showing that stuff or they'll walk out!"

"All right," says Joe, "what're you doing Thursdays?"

"Thursdays," replies Benny, "Thursdays are already taken, that's chinaware night."

On Thursdays, normally a slow night, most of the regular theaters that were competitive would offer a free gift to attract customers. One Thursday night you might get a teacup if it was a chinaware night, then if you went the next week you would get the matching saucer. Ushers would hand them out as you left the theater following the show...

Of course, Joe Pechette's got bigger ideas than that! When Benny says he's giving away china on Thursday night, Joe asks, "How do you give the china away?"

Benny replies, "The ushers just hand it out from a box."

Pechette says, "The Bijou, they don't just give them out. Don't you put them in a bag?"

"No, never," replies Benny, "bags just cost too much!"

"Tell you what," says Pechette, "I will get you bags for all your china if you will tell your projectionist to run our trailer."

"Oh no, no!" cries Benny. "If not," says Joe, "other theaters will get the same idea as the Bijou and you'll be the only one not giving china away in a bag!"

* * * * *

Though by no means a professional cinematographer, Morant had been involved enough to realize the needs and problems of shooting movie footage. In conjunction with photography, he had spent roughly forty years shooting stills on railroad property, so he certainly had an excellent knowledge of what could or could not be done, and what was safe and what was not.

Remembering those days on the movie sets, Nick was fascinated to see how some of the pictures were made...

For instance, in Superman II there's one sequence where the young Superman, as an 18 year-old teenager, has to out run a passenger train to get to the station before his girlfriend arrives. The train is first seen coming along, and Superman is simply walking along when he realizes the train is going to get to the station long before he can. So he puts on the Superman act and starts running.

In fact, he's running at about 30 mph as a 'cherry picker' truck with cameras suspends him by invisible wires to one side (wires that we could obviously see, but did not show up on the film). The boy who played Superman as a teenager spent over two months practicing in New York city, how to run, how to make running look real even though his feet were not touching the ground. It's not an easy trick.

The whole sequence was an interesting one to shoot. In the movie the train is coming along; Superman is running ahead, and then he speeds up. The camera swings right and Superman makes a running leap as you see the train coming straight at you with the headlight on full. Then the camera rises on the crane as the train passes underneath, just as Superman makes his jump across in front of it.

To make the shot, what was done in reality was that the train was backed underneath the camera; the film was run backwards. They put Superman on his harness on the left hand side of the engine as you see it on the screen, and as the train backs out, the camera drops down, so you now see the headlight. The train keeps on backing up and when its clear of the crossing, they dragged Superman across backwards. When the film is reversed, a very exciting illusion is produced, creating a great sequence on the screen.

Even doing it that way, a far less dangerous method, there were risks. Two ambulances and a doctor were on the set at all times while those sequences were being made. The passenger train used in the filming consisted of a CPR passenger locomotive (a General Motors FP7A) and a collection of old retired day coaches, all painted a bright scarlet and lettered as the "Kansas Flyer." At least a hundred "extras" were hired from around Calgary, whose sole purpose was to ride around in the train for a week as passengers...

The engine suited the train well but it looked too good to the movie people. A lot of the technical people with the film were English. The director of photography was English, a man who had made the picture, "A Bridge Too Far." When they got the engine, all beautifully painted, they immediately took it and altered it. The old day coaches that we rented them were so rickety even the toilets leaked around the floor, but they didn't look old enough. They brought in an Englishman whose specialty was to make things look old, to weather signs, vehicles or trains. He spent four days with water colours, syrups and other materials making that `A' unit and the cars look as if they had never been washed in history. The train really looked decrepit and well used, as if it had never been maintained at all.

A problem arose as a result of that Englishman's work. The diesel unit went back to the railroad shops every night. What if someone who knew nothing about the movie work decided to order it washed! "Hey you guys, drop what you're doing and clean up that engine - it looks like hell!"

That would have been disastrous! So I used to go down personally on every shift just to make sure that everyone coming to work knew it was not to be touched. That meant a lot of strange hours getting down to the shops before each shift change. I actually used to go out there at night with my pajamas on underneath my clothes!

One of the things, too, about coordinating, is

that every once in a while you find yourself in a frightful spot, such as with the train we had for the movie "Days of Heaven." The problem stemmed from the company that was producing this movie; they had to have a great deal of public liability to cover the CPR in case the steam locomotive they hired blew up, or someone was accidentally injured at a public grade crossing. In this case the production company couldn't satisfactorily prove to our insurance experts that they were fully insured for what I think was five million dollars, a fairly big figure! I had instructions that on no account was that movie train allowed to move until the CPR's insurance people were satisfied. The movie guys, of course, are great ones. They think they can run over anybody.

They threatened and cajoled me and took me out to dinner. "Come on," they said, "we're just gonna run it down the track a little way, you know." I said I was very sorry, but I just couldn't allow them to do that. It was as much as my job was worth. I told them that the whole matter was of benefit to them as much as anybody, that they had to have the proper insurance, and that was that. And they tried the Assistant Superintendent of course, but got no-where. They were quite mean about it all; they didn't treat us too kindly after that ruckus.

I remember I went out one day after the insurance matter had been settled: they wanted to make a picture of the train crossing the Lethbridge viaduct, and so I took them to a spot. The young fellow who was in charge of the production unit was a relative of investors in the movie, and I suppose this was one of his chances to even the score. When we finished there, he informed me that they were going the other way and that I would have to get back as best I could. I didn't have a car; I'd come out in theirs. So this lad was just trying to get back at me for standing in their way. "Fine," I told him. I had my CPR radio, of course, so all I had to do was call the station and the yardmaster could quite easily send a taxi out to get me. But that fellow didn't think I had any way of returning.

Then an impasse developed. When we were set to go, everybody got in the car but me. They were starting to leave when a Canadian cameraman on the job asked, "What about

Mr.Morant?"

"Oh, he's getting home as best he can," replied the young fellow in charge.

The cameraman got out of his car and went over to him and said, "Look, we're a Canadian group and we're working for you. Mr.Morant is a member of our group even though he may not be a union member, and we are not moving unless Mr.Morant is taken back to where we picked him up!"

So here was a stalemate that I tried to break, but it was of no use; the cameraman would not back down. Finally, they took me back. It was little things like that I'll always remember.

During the movie assignments I worked on, I learned that the thing you must do as the CPR's co-ordinator was to find the director and stick with him. I found I had to stand beside or within hearing distance at all times whether for three days or three months. You couldn't afford to go away for a leak somewhere without telling him you'll be back in a minute, because at any time he might say, "Where's Nick?" and if you're not there, they're not getting what they paid for.

The biggest movie production I co-ordinated was "Silver Streak," which involved the rental of a "Canadian" train set for the better part of six or eight weeks. We ended up in Toronto Union Station with that picture, doing interior shots that involved hundreds of technicians and an incredible number of extras. Since Union Station was not closed down, some 25,000 people a day were going in and out as well, and if any of those people discovered you were an official of the CPR, you started getting an earful of complaints.

There's nothing funnier than to lock a door through which thousands of people pass every afternoon, and when they discover it is locked, they grab the handle and shake it violently as if it were an enemy, thinking it was jammed or something. Then when they find out they really can't go in there, they throw their newspaper down and are terribly upset.

At the end of the day, before the director says, "Well, that'll be a wrap for today!" you had better be right beside him because there's nothing faster than a motion picture company when they break for the day. In twenty minutes there isn't a soul left; you're out there in the middle of the location by yourself. Nobody cares whether you get back home or not, but they sure want you there in the morning!

So I always told the Assistant Superintendent not to go too far away when this guy was getting near quitting time. We needed to know what they were going to do the next day. Once that director got out of your sight, you might spend the rest of the night trying to track him down. They tend to disappear to the most remote restaurants or bars where nobody would obviously look for them.

I would always say, if I were with Arthur Hiller on "Silver Streak," "Well Arthur, what about tomorrow? Which way do you want the train headed?"

On one occasion he said, "East - headed east and we'll be out here about 6.30 or 7.00 tomorrow."

So it was up to me to have the train ready, but as I always made sure the Assistant Superintendent was with me, we'd both write down what the director wanted, because if there was a mistake, the company would be to blame and held responsible for any expense caused by our error.

The next morning everybody arrived and the passenger train was turned the wrong way, but it was the way the director had said. He had indeed said east, but Hiller was not the sort of guy who'd try and pin it on you.

"My goodness," he said, "we'll just have to have it turned then."

To turn it we had to go from Pincher Creek down to Pecten on the Drywood branch and turn the train on the wye. It ended up taking about four hours!

Another sort of thing we were asked to do during the filming of "Silver Streak," for instance, was this: Hiller said, "we want to get a close up of the wheels spinning on the engine."

And as I told Arthur, I said, "Everything known to modern science is now going to conspire against you because these modern engines have a wheel-slip system built on them to prevent just such a thing!"

But we got a chap from motive power who knew what to do. He got some grease and greased down the tracks. That gave us a little bit of a slip, enough to give them the suggestion of the train starting up.

We had one case on "Silver Streak" where we had a special Hollywood signal that caused me no end of problems. I think I made more enemies out of that signal than anything, because one of the CPR's officials had told 20th Century when they first approached the CPR in Vancouver about the movie, that it would be…"Over his dead body"…that Canadian Pacific would operate a train, much less the "Canadian" on his lines. He turned them down quite flatly; the 20th Century production manager was absolutely refused.

The production manager though, being a man of great experience and persuasion, wouldn't be turned off so easily. He went to Montreal and saw Mr.Crump and Mr.Sinclair, and a figure of about two million dollars persuaded the CPR. 20th Century was very impressed with the help that the CPR gave them, and they never ceased to mention that to me. Everybody on the CPR, Glen Swanson and all the public relations people, put their full effort behind it and stayed many more hours than required. I was with them. I worked about 17 hours a day for the best part of three months. The signal problem reappeared, however, when officials in Vancouver, the headquarters of Pacific Region, showed reluctant support for anything to do with this movie.

In the movie, the hero has just vanquished the bad guy, who falls off the train. The bad guy is sent to eternity and the comic lead, scared to death, but who has finally done in the bad guy, turns around to see an overhead signal bridge coming at him - but he's too late to duck!

Here we had a specially gimmicked signal bridge that we located just a few miles east of the McGillivray Loop near the Crowsnest Pass. The movie people in Hollywood had built it. The signal bridge was equipped with roller bearings where the crossarm joined the main upright, and as the hero rushes into the thing and hangs on, the signal bridge swings around and he safely

drops off onto the ground. This was all part of the scenario whereby he is always being dumped off the train. The story revolves around how he keeps getting back on the train even though he is continually falling off, either by his own stupidity or pushed off by the bad guys. Of course, the girl is on the train!

To put up that signal, the Hollywood builders sent me a template of the base showing where the bolts had to be in the concrete foundation we had to build. It was my job to see that the foundation was put in and that the Engineering Department used the template to set the bolts in the proper place on the concrete base.

I had a great deal of trouble with certain officials in the area and finally ended up with a face up battle wherein I had actually to threaten a senior officer in that district that I would take the matter to the President. The local officers were only repeating what higher regional authorities had said. I pointed out to them, however, that no matter what anyone in Vancouver said, they were stuck with this thing and so was I, and that signal was going in! 20th Century paid dearly for what they got, and our job was to give them their money's worth! Finally, we got it in and it worked very well, but no thanks to some of my friends in Pacific Region offices.

* * * * *

"Days of Heaven" was a beautifully photographed movie about life amongst migrant grain harvesters of the 1900s, sort of a period picture. The CPR gave access to our tracks from south of Lethbridge down into the Cardston area. A twenty mile branch from near Cardston went southeast to Whiskey Gap, a small border community consisting of a couple of houses and two grain elevators.

The train the movie company got together consisted of a CNR steam engine from the Alberta Historical Society in Edmonton. We provided only one of the cars in the train; it was an old beat up caboose from the Medicine Hat yard that appeared as if transients had been sleeping in it for some time. The engine operated on its own under steam, but in order to help things along and make sure we didn't get stalled anywhere, we put on a yard diesel at the head end. I remember that it was the only time that I ever saw a train powered with a steam engine and a diesel absolutely stuck hopelessly in Russian thistles and weeds. Both engines stalled because as they tried to plow through, they ground the weeds to a pulp, making the rails extremely slippery. The line hadn't been used for sometime, usually only a few times in the fall, as there was nothing else there except the grain elevators. I believe they have since lifted the track.

They uncoupled the diesel, backed the train out of the way with the steam engine, then made a couple of runs at the weeds with the diesel, finally busting through. It was sort of ridiculous to see this train stuck on a piece of track that had been so disused that the weeds were stronger than the engines.

In one of the scenes in "Days of Heaven" the train is about to leave Whiskey Gap, taking with it a lot of migrant workers riding on the roofs of cars or anywhere else they could find. On this train, strangely, they had of all these old freight cars and an auxiliary crane. When I saw this, I wondered what in the hell do they want an auxiliary crane on what is apparently a regularly scheduled freight train. Hollywood's answer was, "Well, when they were up in Edmonton they saw this crane and it looked sort

Canadian National ten wheeler (a 2-6-0 built in 1913) No.1392 and the "hodge-podge" of equipment collected from the Alberta Pioneer Railway Association for the shooting of the movie "Days of Heaven," passes by the elevators at Whiskey Gap, Alberta, on CPR's Woolford Subdivision branch line. Morant made the photograph while assigned as the CPR's co-ordinator for the movie production, a job that entailed synchronizing the crews and support staff that the CPR supplied under contract during filming in 1979. *NMC*

ALBERTA
WHEAT POOL
FARMER OWNED
CO-OPERATIVE
WHISKY GAP

of cute!"

It looked better than a boxcar so they sent it along. Of course, it had to be hauled at 20 mph all the way down from Edmonton, so it took quite a while, but nonetheless we got it down there.

Anyway, the scene is the elevators at dusk and is what is known in photography as a picture made at the mystic hour and though nobody really knows what that time is, it comes late on a summer's evening when there's just enough light to give you an exposure of the landscape without getting too much else. The photographer of this movie was well known for his beautiful effects, so he had to call the exact time he wanted the shot made.

With the engine and train behind us out of the scene, we are looking at the elevators. The track runs straight out past the elevator to a point about 300 yards beyond and that's the end of the track, so we can't get the train going too fast or we'll derail it. It had to be done very carefully, but it also had to be timed well because in the scene the leading lady is initially sitting in the grass, but when she hears the whistle of the train, she has to get up and run across the field toward the train. There's a camera dolly track a few hundred feet long. When she says, "I've got to go, the train is coming," the camera follows her as she runs across the field. As she's running ahead the train comes into the side of the screen so the shot has to be perfectly timed.

You can't start up a steam engine as you can a diesel, so you have to figure out how long it'll take them to start up and get to that point. Long before the leading lady is ready to go, you have to give the train the cue to proceed. The engineer slowly gets under way, and finally has a little speed. He has to be coming by with a certain box car exactly at the right time, and for some reason or another it fell on me to cue the engineer. I had no idea how it would work out. It was going to take a lot of luck, but the director and the photographer agreed that they would have to try to do it right at the first attempt as there might not be enough light to do it a second time.

Everybody on set knew that this was an important shot, so a certain tenseness pervaded the scene. The gal, the train, the director and

photographer were all ready. "OK, cue the train!" I told the engineer, who was Jack Hewitson, over the radio. He started up the track, and the girl started to run. Now what I have to tell you is that the girl, a very beautiful creature, came right off the streets of Brooklyn, as I was told by one of the American cameramen. Her language, he had said, was not always the best! She started her run. Earlier she had been needling the director to get rid of the high-button shoes she wore that had to be laced with a hook. They dated back to the styles at the turn of the century and were uncomfortable and painful to her. Of course, there's no way the director was going to allow her to wear anything else in case the camera should pick up the discrepancy. She was grudgingly made to wear them.

So now she's running in the scene. The camera's moving along beside her, everything is going well, the train is right on the spot at the right time, and just as she gets near the railway track, she falls flat on her nose. Tumbling over, there she lay, and she knew what had happened, she knew that she had blown an important shot. If this shot isn't gotten tonight, they will have to wait until the next night. A whole crew of a hundred people another night in the hotel, more meals and other expenses. So everyone knows, everyone's all keyed up on getting this shot.

Amidst the shouting, "Cut! Cut!" she gets back up. I stop the train and tell the engineer immediately to back up to the starting point as something has gone wrong. Dusting off her clothes, the girl gets up and points her finger at the director, screaming, "Jack, you son-of-a-bitch, you and your frigging shoes!"

Portfolio VI

Canadian Pacific Hotels

Canadian Pacific's chefs are among the finest artisans of their trade in the world. *NMC*

The Chateau Frontenac in Quebec City. *NMC*

Tea at the Empress Hotel in Victoria, British Columbia. *NMC*

Yachts anchored in the Inner Harbour at the foot of the Empress Hotel grounds in Victoria. *NMC*

Conference room in the Chateau Frontenac, Quebec City. *CPCA*

Ballroom in the Royal York Hotel, Toronto, Ontario. *CPCA*

The grounds of the Chateau Lake Louise, taken from the roof of the east wing. *NMC*

The Chateau Lake Louise east wing and the swimming pool in the foreground, Canadian Pacific's most elegant hotel in the most beautiful location. Next to Niagara Falls, it is the most popular honeymoon retreat in Canada. *NMC*

The Banff Springs Hotel and golf course, along the Bow River, seen from Tunnel Mountain. *NMC*

CHAPTER ELEVEN

Encounters With Mr.Crump and Other CPR Officials

It was natural, considering Nick Morant's position as Special Photographer for Public Relations, that sooner or later he would have dealings with those in the top echelons of the Canadian Pacific Railway. Morant's career spanned fifty years, less the four he spent with the Winnipeg Free Press. He began at the time Sir Edward Beatty reigned as President and Chairman of the Board. He retired when Ian D. Sinclair was Chairman and Fred Burbidge, President. Over the period of his career, he served under nine different Presidents of the CPR.

Some of the top people lasted only a few years, but others like Sir Edward Beatty were there for what often seemed interminable lengths of time. Norris R. Crump was in top office for some eighteen years and was a well esteemed and decisive leader. During Nick Morant's career a profound mutual respect grew between the two men as both were outspoken and refused to beat around the bush. Both were practical men who tended to believe common sense should rule in all matters, and both had a mutual hobby - steam engineering...

Sir Edward was, when I joined the CPR in 1929, Chairman of the Board, and President. This guy, you know, he was 'God' around there! You contrast Sir Edward with Mr.Crump, for instance. Sir Edward lived on Pine avenue, the locale for homes of CPR higher executives, and Mr.Crump, well he lived in one of the nicer middle class suburbs of Montreal. He never changed his place of residence as he climbed the ladder.

I know someone who was coming up an alley in a heavy snowstorm when he got stuck. A Mercedes-Benz came up behind him and the driver signalled him to get in the car and he'd push him. The Mercedes pushed him out and away he went. He waved to the man, only to recognize N.R.Crump, ever the practical man. Still a machinist at heart, which was the profession he rose from, he always drove his own car. Very rarely did he use the company limousine and driver, except for special occasions.

In one of my first encounters with Mr.Crump, he was a Senior Vice-President at the time, we had decided that in order to get photographs required by Publicity of modern passenger trains in the mountains, we were going to have to run a special train. The advertising people in the States, particularly, needed photographs to produce the sort of illustrations that would compare the CPR's passenger service to that of the famous streamliners on the Great Northern and Santa Fe then being introduced. It was decided, in Montreal, in conjunction with Mr.Crump, that a train of what was then modern style, clean passenger equipment, would be run out west and we would have it for three days.

In the initial stages everything was handled from Montreal, and then as plans were formulated and finalized the authority moved west when the train was sent out from Montreal's Glen yard. The train was destined for Calgary and we were to photograph between there and Field, so all our orders eventually trickled down to the Superintendent responsible for the Alberta Division. Back in Montreal, Mr.Crump, it seems, had made a suggestion that of the three days the train was to run, one would be the 24th of May, the Victoria Day holiday!

We had laid plans for the movie crew to shoot footage looking back on the passenger train rounding mountain curves by positioning them in a flange-wheeled automobile, which in those days was a Buick, and running the Buick 150 yards or so ahead of the train. It didn't mean much for the stills we were doing, but by removing the back window of the car the movie boys were able to get some spectacular footage. This footage was to be shot down around Gap Lake, and the train was to come into the mountains with the camera leading the train around the corner as they shot from the car, then they'd open the camera up on the mountain background as the train headed west.

This was a hazardous shot because if the automobile were to stall, there was no way the train could stop short. If it hit them, it would almost surely kill somebody! So we didn't like the idea of shooting on the 24th of May holiday; we didn't want to take the risk of having people gathered along the railway track cheering the automobile on as it went by, simply because we'd have a whole crowd of people around we couldn't control. A meeting was held in Calgary at the Division offices, where I strongly voiced my opposition. We just couldn't do something like that around Banff on May 24th without attracting crowds.

But the Superintendent said to me, "Well, Mr.Morant, this is Mr.Crump's suggestion. The next matter before the meeting, gentlemen, is ...." So I was ignored.

By good fortune, another one of my famous meetings where `the tide is turned,' occurred at the Palliser Hotel in Calgary where I was billeted. I was wondering how the hell we were going to manage this business, but there seemed nothing I could do as the situation was out of my hands, when whom do I see at the newsstand at that moment but `Brother Crump!' He was still only a Vice-President, but big enough to be of help to me.

When he saw me he said, "How are you getting along with that train?" I replied, "Well sir, everything's going pretty good, but this

This low angle view of the special passenger train assembled for publicity shots on the Laggan Subdivision in the "Canadian Pacific Rockies," was made by Morant on the curve at mileage 113.0 that is better known as Morant's Curve. The photograph was made on the morning of May 25, 1952 as the photo crews worked their way eastward back toward Banff and Calgary. This is one of the photographs that turned out fine, thanks to Morant's foresight in using old as well as new, film holders. *NMC*

business of running on the 24th of May is a bad mistake!"

Crump immediately took offence at this. "Well, I made the suggestion that you run it on that day because you're on work train orders; you're going to have to get out of the way of everything moving on those tracks. I thought it would be easier for you guys!"

"Mr. Crump, do you remember when you were Master Mechanic at Wilkie, Saskatchewan?"

"Yes," he replied, "What the hell's that got to do with this?"

"Well, sir, just this. You know damned well that if the Senior Vice-President of this organization makes a suggestion in Montreal, it comes out of the Superintendent's office here as a

bloody order, right?"

"Well, run the bloody train whenever you want!" he said.

That was probably the first instance that I recall an encounter with Norris R. Crump.

Little did Mr. Crump realize how close we came to disaster on that one. Because I am a bit of a worrier, I thought to myself I'd better not trust my old plate holders on a job like this. I decided that I would buy a couple of dozen new 5 x 7 holders from the Lisco Corporation in Los Angeles, who were big producers of plate holders - in fact, I think, the only ones in the world now. I ordered two dozen of those things; that gave me enough holders for 48 shots, plus as many again of the older ones. So I went out mostly with new

plate holders, but I didn't want to put all my eggs in one basket. Perhaps the new ones might leak light too, who knows! If you had a plate holder that leaked any light, you would get a picture that was useless.

We made the pictures with some of the new holders as well as the old ones. We made our still pictures as well as motion pictures, and finally, the day came when the train was released and sent back. I managed a very difficult thing; I developed some of the pictures right away in a colour lab set up in a bath tub in the Palliser Hotel. This was the only time in my career I did this, and it worked, but I wouldn't want to do it continuously. You have tolerances of plus or minus a half a degree and that includes your running water -you can't be off.

Portfolio VII

Canadian Pacific Air Lines

Douglas DC-3s, the primary and most popular postwar airliner in North America, were the mainstay of Canadian Pacific's fleet for many years. Here two of the fleet of 17 DC-3s await their passengers and mail before departing Vancouver, one to Prince Rupert, the other to Calgary, shortly after the Canadian Government awarded those route licenses to CPAL in the fall of 1947. *NMC*

Two ground crewmen are loading mail into the front baggage door of this Canadian Pacific DC-3 as it prepares for departure in front of the old Vancouver Airport terminal, circa 1947. *NMC*

In an air to air photograph, Morant made this picture of a Canadian Pacific Air Lines DC-3 over the City of Montreal in 1947. Directly below the cockpit is Canadian Pacific headquarters and Windsor Street station, below the tail is the Jacques Cartier bridge and the Port of Montreal on the St.Lawrence River. *NMC*

For services to the four corners of the globe, the prime goal of Canadian Pacific's President, former bush pilot Grant McConachie; CPAL needed long range ocean spanning airliners. They were not available till after the conclusion of World War II, but aircraft builder Donald Douglas designed and built the DC-4 for just such services.

Canadair in Montreal needed new peacetime projects to maintain their skilled staff and profits, so they contracted to license-build the DC-4 at Cartierville with some modifications. They substituted the Pratt and Whitney Twin Wasp radial engines for the Rolls Royce Merlin in-line engines of World War II fame. The aircraft was labelled the Canadair Four, better known by its RCAF name "North Star".

Morant made photographs of the brand new Empress of Vancouver off the coast of British Columbia for use in company ads. The aircraft's registration is CF-CPR and was the second of four C-4s, delivered in 1949. *NMC*

Resplendent in perfect light as it cruised over the Gulf Islands, Canadair Four, the Empress of Vancouver showed off its fine lines for Morant's cameras. CF-CPR flew until 1950 when it was written off in a landing accident at Tokyo airport. The Rolls Royce engines were noted for their noise and appetite for fuel. The aircraft was likened to "a flight of Spitfires in very close formation." *NMC*

The <u>Empress of Sydney,</u> a <u>Canadair Four,</u> is on the ramp at Vancouver with three lovely ladies dressed for a flight to Australia (note the hat boxes). This aircraft, CF-CPI, made the first scheduled flight to Australia via San Francisco, Honolulu, and Fiji in 39 hours with two overnight stops during July of 1949, inaugurating a fortnightly service. September saw the inauguration of weekly flights on the lucrative route to Tokyo via Anchorage and Shemya in the Aleutians. *NMC*

CF-CPX, a DC-3 purchased by Canadian Pacific Air Lines in 1943, overflies the agrarian countryside south of Montreal, in an air to air publicity pose for the cameras of Nick Morant, circa 1947. *NMC*

The Douglas DC-6B, the first true long range airliner, purchased by CPAL in 1953, was a very profitable aircraft for Grant McConachie's airline. Twenty, of various configurations, flew for the airline until 1968, allowing CPA to establish routes to South America (in 1953) and Europe (in 1955).

To train crews, a DC-6B simulator was purchased for the crew training base at Vancouver Airport on Sea Island. For the Spanner, Canadian Pacific's in house magazine, Morant wrote an article about the new simulator and made the accompanying photograph. The cockpit is up front beyond the two instructor/examiners who control all the inputs into the machinery to simulate flight, abnormal situations and emergencies. *NMC*

Two brand new Bristol Britannias occupy Canadian Pacific Air Line's new Britannia hangar at Vancouver. Morant photographed the <u>Empress of Vancouver</u> and the <u>Empress of Hong Kong</u> days after their arrival from the Bristol factory in England in April, 1958. *NMC*

Eight 400mph long range turbo-prop Bristol Britannias, touted as the "Whispering Giants," were purchased to replace DC-6Bs until jetliners became available. They were a beautiful aircraft but their reliability suffered, largely due to electrical problems. In this night scene Morant photographed the Britannias through the hangar doors at Vancouver in 1958. *NMC*

Self portrait, a photograph made by Willie. *NMC*

CHAPTER TWELVE
Letters to the Editor

One of Morant's longest and closest friendships is with Colin Haworth and his wife Nora of Montreal. Haworth joined the CPR in 1938 as a press writer and first met Morant shortly thereafter when Nick was in Montreal doing hotel and tourist shots. They immediately 'cottoned' to one another because of a similar sense of humor and became great friends. Haworth didn't remain long with the CPR; he went on to bigger public relations companies and ventures, but they remained close friends, exchanging correspondence interminably, partaking in many practical jokes and financial schemes.

On one occasion early in their friendship, Haworth was traveling the CPR to Vancouver on business, when he wired Morant in Kamloops from Regina, just for some fun. The message said nothing more than to wave as the train went through town. Late at night, in pouring rain, the passenger train made a ten-minute stop at Kamloops. Haworth was restless and stepped off for some fresh air. Who was there on the platform but Morant himself riding a bicycle, beside him on a horse was Molly, Morant's mother! What a sight!

Most of Haworth's recollections reflect their mutual belief that humor is a great and necessary part of life, a relief valve for pent up tensions and troubles in the work place and at home. That was their common bond, that life, no matter how serious or desperate, always had its lighter side. Laughter and good humor dulls the sharp edge of seriousness and brings warmer meaning to the attentions of work. So they mutually became involved in schemes and scams that usually ended up as jokes upon themselves; sometimes they got into hot water, but mostly a great laugh was had and no harm done.

The 'Coolbrook Symphony' was one of those lighter sides of life that Morant and Haworth partook of. To imply that either was a classical musician would be unwise, although they both owned instruments of quality and played with great enthusiasm - Morant a flute, and Haworth a guitar.

The 'orchestra' requires some explanation. It dates back to the 40's. Its members were generally in writing, art, or photography for the purposes of making a living. With few exceptions none could read music (those that did would deny it and in any event could read only slowly and inaccurately). But all of them played. They played, with love and abandon, the popular music of the preceding 30 years. Into an ensemble like this Morant and his flute fit perfectly. The others all played so loudly he could miss five notes out of ten and no one would be any the wiser.

Not all members of the 'symphony' owned their instruments. Some were borrowed. The return of those instruments was often regretfully delayed or even overlooked. Once, a piano remained on the 'borrowed' status for about 25 years before the owner tracked it down. A bassoon appeared that had no reed, necessitating a late night call on the senior bassoonist of the Ottawa Symphony Orchestra to borrow one. It was 'late night' because that was when most of the Coolbrook's 'guessed' performances were held. There were occasions when the audiences were joined by uniformed police officers investigating complaints of neighbors who had not the wit to join in the rumble, uninvited but welcome.

Morant, who was one of the founding fathers of this institution, has a special niche in its archives. He named the group! Prior to that it had just been a matter of jam sessions at a duplex on Coolbrook Avenue in Montreal. Through his and others' constant travelling, the group expanded across North America.

If you happened to hear the 'Overture to William Tell' being played on four tin whistles at 2am in the corridors of the Empress Hotel in Victoria about 42 years ago, you have participated as an Honorary Associate Listening Member. Same thing if you walked by the old Canadian Press office in Halifax at five in the morning one historic night and heard two trumpets and one trombone giving virtuoso performances of 'The Twelfth Street Rag,' a performance that ended only as the lead player slid gently down the post he was leaning against, and passed out on the floor.

Morant and one of the other founding fathers of the 'Coolbrook Symphony' were sticklers for equal rights. Nowhere, even in the Soviet Union, has egalitarianism reached such heights. They determined from the start that all membership cards should carry the number one - not just printed on the cards, which would look artificial, but added by an automatic numbering machine. The printer who had to keep turning his numbering device back after each impression, was upset. And a few minor brawls may have occurred on occasion, when members who had not been notified of the system, met in some strange city, proudly exchanged their No.1 cards, then clashed briefly.

It is a recorded event that the 'Coolbrook Symphony' was the first orchestra ever to play in the 3000 seat opera house of the National Art Centre in Ottawa. Moreover it was, on a later engagement, the first ensemble (of its kind) to be brought up on the Centre's rising stage. Maintenance staff had to be paid extra to do this. It is only an aside to note that in this second performance the 'Symphony' was joined by an Ottawa Conservatory type who, hearing the fun from behind the curtain, could not restrain himself and slipped discreetly onto the stage to participate. He had the good grace to play his clarinet rather than his flute.

Haworth and Morant kept up an ongoing correspondence through the years, letters that often joked about their personal experiences, family problems and work related disputes. Full of their mutually shared sense of humor, these letters often, as well, took up causes (sometimes ridiculous) that they championed. That would, in turn, result in a flurry of letters to various companies, governments or editors complaining, cajoling or downright criticizing the situation. They sometimes got into trouble that way, but often they made new friends, and even, in one instance, brought justice to a public cause.

The worst pranks that Morant and Haworth played were upon each other. Morant started it! He clipped a coupon registering Haworth in the "Toledo School of Meat Cutting." You can imagine the amount of correspondence Haworth got on that one - it went on for years!

They kept this kind of thing going endlessly. The best one Haworth got on Morant was when he found an application form for the "Banff School of Advanced Management Training," which he promptly filled out with Morant's name.

The last question on the form was, "Give reasons why you should be admitted to the Banff School of Advanced Management Training."

Haworth wrote, "There are times when I'm across the river taking passport photos (the Banff School of Fine Arts is across the Bow River from Morant's home) that I get caught short due to the trouble I had with a bear a few years ago. It is at times like this I'd like to be admitted to the Banff School of Management Training rather than drive all the way home in distress."

No doubt everyone in Banff heard about that!

Years ago there was a magazine called

The Reporter, from New York, that Haworth used to read. It contained reprints of things from all over - it was a real "insider" magazine. They had an ad about themselves that they used to run once in a while, that was based on people keeping things from you. The heading was "The Zone of Silence." It elaborated on the so-called Juan de Fuca Straits zone-of-silence story with mysterious sunken ships lying on the sea bottom.

The two friends would operate as a team on things like this. Haworth wrote a letter to the magazine with a copy sent to Morant. Morant would respond immediately, writing in support of Haworth's complaint. They forced them, just out of logic, because Morant took the time to dig up letters and correspondence from marine experts in British Columbia, to stop using their ridiculous advertisement. The magazine people were quite amused by all this, and finally wrote back saying, "OK, OK, you guys win!"

This business of sending each other carbon copies enlisting each other in battles of nonsensical, sometimes ridiculous, and always humorous matters nearly got Haworth into a tight squeeze once. With another friend, Haworth had been digging around in an old second-hand store and had found several large-sized Thomas Birch paintings. (He was famous for the picture of the naval battle between the USS Constitution and the French war ship Guerriere in which John Paul Jones became famous.) He was the first major marine artist in the United States. Haworth spent a lot of time getting the paintings cleaned up, photographed, and researched. It turned out that they were of some minor value.

Then they set about selling them. They went after Knodler's, the biggest art dealer in New York, on 57th Street. Haworth wrote a letter indicating he was thinking of breaking up his art collection - would they be interested? He intimated that he was a famous collector, when between friends they only had three old Birch paintings. A

reply came back from Knodler's explaining that Mr.Knodler was in France at the moment, but would be back next month and would undoubtedly get in touch.

Haworth then drafted a letter, signed by his secretary, explaining that Haworth was in Banff, Alberta, at the time, but on returning, he would be informed that Mr.Knodler was interested in his collection.

A little trick to impress the recipients of letters is to put `cc' (carbon copy) at the bottom with affixed names. Haworth used Messr.Willie Chevalier and Nicholas E.Morant, but using the latter proved a big mistake. Even though he told his secretary not to send any copies, she forgot the warning and did!

About a week later Haworth received a carbon copy from Morant of a letter he had sent to Knodler's explaining that Haworth was no where to be found and that he was last seen on the roof of a train just before it entered the Connaught Tunnel. Morant thought this was another of their mutual games and was willing to play it to the hilt, but all Haworth was trying to do was sell those three paintings. After some long-winded explanations, they were sold to Knodler's for $2000.00, but those people must have wondered what-in-the-devil was going on with this fellow Haworth. And who-in-the-hell was Morant!

This letter writing business all stemmed from Morant's earlier experiences in the Public Relations Department of the CPR in Montreal. He was influenced by a group of PR men who made it their business to write letters to the editors, influencing newspapers and their policies toward the CPR. In the department there was an old gentleman by the name of C.W.Lane. He was a man who was well spoken and could read and write five different languages. He seemed quite out of place there, and although he was assigned the task of translating letters for the law department at times, his main task was to clip the newspapers of the country for the use of Public Relations, which influenced company policy by keeping officers informed of happenings over the system. In that group there were others, including a fellow named Rolley O'Leary, Morant, and of all people, Percy Cole, who was a New York public relations man for the CPR, and a great sport. Cole originally worked for the Toronto <u>Telegram</u>, and his son, whom Morant knew well, was a photographer at the <u>Telegram.</u>

Nick recalls how things would often develop...

We were professional writers of letters-to-the-editor and it would all start this way, as one did: I remember it well, I was there. Old man Lane, a nice little fellow with an English accent, very well heeled, far better educated than even his bosses, would say to O'Leary; "Rolley, you know we haven't had any letters to the editor lately, have we? Nearly a month since we've done anything!"

Rolley would reply, "You're right, C.W. What do you think we should do?"

Lane would stretch out, then scratch his side. "I don't know. How about dogs in the park! That's always good for a row!"

So it would start: everybody would begin writing letters about dogs in the park. Then letters from dog-lovers would flow into the papers crying unfair. Then pretty soon letters would show up from New York lamenting on the similar problems of their parks.

Of course, this was Percy Cole at work! He would fan the fire further by writing anonymous letters from fictitious characters in support of one side or the other.

In this strange way they would manipulate public opinion on many issues, and if the subject could be carried to the CPR, then away they would go. At times they even wrote letters opposing CPR policy in order to force company officials to modify their position! It was never beyond a guy like Cole to criticise company policy in this way; he was never beyond giving the company a going over if he thought he could bring some sense to CPR officials.

This all brings up a story involving Morant and an osprey, an animal story if you like, but one that brought a happy ending for all, including the CPR, who received great PR over the matter. An osprey, as most of you know, is a bird of prey, also known as a sea eagle, but is of the hawk family and feeds entirely on fish. Nests are established at the tops of dead trees, or on power or telephone poles near the water's edge, and are used year after year. This story that I shall let Morant tell in his own words, resulted from exhaustive letters-to-the-editor, written by Morant...

I was having coffee with George Scott, the CPR lineman at Banff, down at the station news-stand one day, and he said to me; "Those bloody ospreys, they're getting into everything. I've got a nest out there that I'm going to knock over one of these days."

I said, "You're in a National Park, for heaven's sake, you can't just go and dump those birds out of their nests!"

"We gotta', the nest gets wet, then we get line losses, signals start going to ground and you get all kinds of noises on the wire too."

I asked him, "Are you going to do that very soon, because I'd like you to leave it as long as you can, maybe I can get a picture of it."

Picture! Horse shit, I thought to myself. I'd already started to save that nest if I could. "All right Nick," replied George, "I'll hold on."

I knew George Scott; he was a man to leave till next Tuesday something that could be done Monday. He wasn't inclined to bust his ass! He was prepared to work at all times of night or day, but when it came to removing osprey nests, he wasn't in any hurry.

I figured it was no use doing anything but going public on this! It was the era when you could write a letter to a newspaper and not have to give your real name. You could just write any normal address and no one would bother checking, but since people are now being sued for everything, the papers have adopted a very careful policy. Now they check out every letter they print, determining if there is, in fact, a bonafide person at that address. But they didn't do that at the time I'm speaking of, so I wrote a letter to the <u>Calgary Herald.</u> I complained of the fact that the CPR and National Parks would

allow such a travesty of nature, the dumping of an osprey and her chicks out of their nest unceremoniously. I complained it was a crime and a total shame that such a thing could happen and that somebody should speak up for those birds. That started it!

Many other people began writing in to the Herald, and I myself wrote other letters from other fictitious characters backing up my original letter.

"Get after these bastards!" I wrote. "Heartless, cruel!" I penned.

Then one day the door bell rang. It was a fellow by the name of Graham Nichols from the local Public Relations office of the CPR in Banff. He had with him Ken Liddell, a well read columnist from the Calgary Herald newspaper, who wrote a sort of folksy column about country folk and rural happenings in Alberta. These two men came on in and I made them tea.

"Had I ever taken any pictures of the osprey nest along the railway west of Banff here?" Nichols asked.

I replied, "Yes, I just happen to have some here in my files. Why would you be asking?"

"Well," said Nichols, "I guess you haven't heard about it, but there's one hell of a row going on about this George Scott and that nest, people phoning us and the Herald continuously. Ken's been sent up here to see if he can run this thing down and find out what it's all about."

I told them that what it was all about was pretty simple. Poor George Scott who's got a job to do has been told to tear that nest down. In Holland they erect scaffolding just for the storks to nest in, on telegraph poles and roof tops. That way they don't interfere with anything. I would think myself that in order to save us a lot of trouble, somebody should just tell George to put up another cross arm and move the nest up on it, that's all they'd have to do.

Then my guests said, "We're trying to find the person that wrote that letter in the first place. You wouldn't have any ideas would you?"

"Wasn't it some woman, Agnes somebody or other?" I said.

"That's right," replied Nichols, "but nobody knows the woman or where she lives."

"That's strange!" I said, and in the corner of my eye I could see the typewriter that those

letters were written on, practically right in front of them!

George Scott was simply doing his job without too much thought, and Canadian Pacific was quite interested in saving the ospreys, despite what seemed an unfeeling order at first. Morant made pictures of them saving the nest. It ended up appearing in Ripley's "Believe It or Not" and became good copy in many newspapers all over. Afterwards, Canadian Pacific made a permanent home for those birds, just as had been done for the storks in Holland centuries before...

It was a thing that I was pleased with because it didn't hurt anybody, says Morant, but nothing would have saved that nest if I hadn't written that letter!

In the course of preparing the manuscript for this book, I approached Nick Morant on the methods of photography in the days of flash powder. His reply was received in letter-to-the-editor form in January of 1989. It is hereby copied unedited, for your amusement...

THIS IS "LETTERS to EDITOR DAY."

Dear Sir,

Would someone mind explaining to me just what it is the so-called old fashioned photographer is supposed to be doing in the line repro bottom left corner of Rail News Volume 1 Number 769298. ???

First off - with but one minor exception the artist could be depicting most of the serious photographers at work in this Anno Dom 1987. The old fashioned camera depicted here is quite modern. The tripod of insufficient build for such a camera is also modern.

The cameraman raises some questions. Is he about to be seated in a public lavatory? Awaiting possibly some homo sexual advances

from a passing 35mm camera enthusiast? What is he holding aloft with his right hand? I assume it is an old style flash "pan" ... where we get the melodious sounds of the catch phrase "He's only a flash in the pan".... explosions of this sort were not uncommon ... two ounces of magnesium powder could put a cameraman out of business - often for life, through blindness.

I think the artist is just all wrong. If you seek advice from the Geriatric Ward in the County Home for Aged Cameramen (in Toronto) you would find that my words are spoken with forked tongue but true ...

1. *As you can see, I now have time to write silly letters full of jokes (??) Forget 2 and 3 ...*

The method shown in this illustration are about as accurate as a photo of a 5900 without a booster. Let me elucidate. May I? Thankyou sir - tell that kid to stand back or he'll get a bash in the face from ME.

You beat your subject into insensibility .. then

1. *focus the camera*
2. *go under cloth*
       and find you've not set the shutter on time ...
3. *Come out from under the cloth and focus.*
       to find that you've forgotten to open the iris on the shutter
4. *Come out from under the camera and change iris (Margaret is better)*
5. *Go back under the cloth and focus and compose shot*
       only to find the tripod screw isn't holding the camera tightly meaning you have to make a cardboard shim ..
6. *You are now half way ready to proceed*
       in this day and age you'd go to coffee

7. *You are about ready for the nitty. You get a slide loaded with a glass plate.*

8. *You close the iris*
9. *Set the shutter from T to B*
       find you've not put on the cable release

10. *Put on the cable release*

11. *Make a test of the release and shutter*

12. *Tell your subject you are almost ready*
       find out you're not sure how well the shutter was working

13. *Make a fresh test*

14. *Ask the subject if he has any last words to say to the world.*

14.a *Ask the owner of a nearby barking dog to quiet the animal or you'll kick it in the guts ... dogs have a habit of howling when death is present - upsetting difficult subjects who have ill fitting dentures.*
14.b *Place film holder upon which you have been standing since item 7 (See above somewhere) in the back of the camera.*
14.c *Gingerly remove safety slide - keeping it underneath the focusing cloth to prevent an almost hundred percent chance of fogging the film some where along the way.*
14.d *Be sure to place safety slide somewhere handy ... a pocket? No ... no pockets will hold an 8x Film Holder..... Don't give it to a little boy, he will make a sail boat out of it before you can reach him (or the boat) ... set it on top of the camera ... that way the wind will blow it down and you can stand on it as in*

section (Item 14.b) 14.e SEE SPECIAL INSTRUCTIONS as below .. done in rapid fire manner ...

88.c   Reach for two ounce bottle of Magnesium Powder. Place a generous amount on the flash pan holder -AFTER having transferred it from the bottle to a slip of paper .... in a 12 mph wind. Each photographer had his own formula of how much of the bloody powder was required to properly expose a plate at a given distance ... some people allowed a little extra because it was 1. An exterior flash 2. A 12 mph wind was gonna' blow away half the "charge" - don't forget ...

88.d   don't forget to make sure the subject isn't asleep .... NOW transfer the powder to the flash pan (yes, in the wind, how else canya do it?) you think you have troubles with electronic flashes passing out after the 8th exposure only to find they test out as strong ....?

88.e   Now, quickly, you transfer the powder onto the flash pan. You grab the shutter release cable and begin wondering whether you changed the iris to f8 ... did you check the T and B settings ? Where is the safety slide holder? ... one thing you did learn ... you're standing on it - something's going well ...

88.f   Warn the subject ... steady now. He opens his eyes -he knows there's gonna be a blinding flash ... but you have him by the nuts YOU know when its coming, eh? The subject reflects sheer and absolute terror, the sort of look you get

when you give them a North Korean Water Torture.

88.g   The wind velocity is increasing, another five seconds and there won't be any powder on the flash unit. You open the shutter with one hand, give a hasty look at how much dust is in the pan, YOU PULL THE FLASH RELEASE.

nothing happens.

88.h   The subject has gone down under the stress. There is just so much even the strongest of men can accept —if you discount those who stuttered forever after this Inquisitorial Demonstration. I know of instances where it was the photographer who stuttered.

You call the ambulance who take away the horrible gibbering mess that was once a man - a human being ... well, like yourself for instance. What powder you had in the pan has long since gone into the Valley of the Dolls ... lost forever ... and no loss either. The reason why the flash didn't operate was that you had forgotten Item 88.z ... which reads in part ..."Make sure that you wind the clockwork mechanism which actuates a spark producing phenomena which, like oldtime cigarette lighters, ignites the powder."

You are finished for the evening ...... a second shot to do inside, did you say? A banquet, did you say?? Here is your chance to get even with society. Follow all rules up to and including 88.h ... everything man ... that includes the iris setting, T - B setting - did you actually focus this one or was it the last? (Incidentally where the hell is that safety slide ... eh, you found it, eh? Sticking to your boot with some Wrigley's Chewing Gum on it?)

... So you go through all the agony all over ... with two hundred people watching you and you're worried about the blind photographers and making with the gags and being the funny

man ... ("There's my friend - old Foote himself", so said Edward - Prince of Wales when he visited Winnipeg on one occasion to find the lean old gentleman waiting with his 8x10 for an official photo ... nearly always showing more quality than all the photos made by other cameramen on the assignment.)

... Be brief sir, will you? Certainly ... call the meeting to order please. Everybody at this banquet please turn your chair so you can SEE the camera lens ... that way you'll know you're in the picture ... everybody steady ... one two three KAMBLOOMIE. The flash goes off successfully like a rocket at Canaveral ... well almost every time ... NOW is the time for the getaway in a minute or so the smoke will come, raining down ashes on everybody's head, and all over the table cloths etc. etc. Photographers who were caught before they could leave the hotel banquet room met some awful deaths ..... one, I knew well as a friend, was sent in a box to the crater of Krakatoa and there deposited to await the day the extinct volcano erupted with a crash which went around the world .... the photographers lot is not an 'appy one.

Signed

Marantz

An old mariner never retires. *NMC*

Portfolio VIII

Portraits

J.A. Walker, retired CPR locomotive engineer, Thunder Bay, Ontario, photographed by Morant for <u>The Spanner</u> on the occasion of Mr. Walker's 101st birthday. *NMC*

At Cominco's Sullivan mine at Kimberley, B.C., miners posed in the underground caverns of the lead-zinc mine in 1965. Cominco is an acronym for Consolidated Mining and Smelting Company, a subsidiary of Canadian Pacific that was sold amidst great criticism from "Wall Street" in the downsizing of CP during the 1990s. *CPCA*

The Morant's at work. *NMC*

The results. *NMC*

Self portrait of Nick and Willie in Nova Scotia, made by Morant. The remote release cable extends from Nick's hands out of the picture at the bottom of the frame. *NMC*

CHAPTER 13
The Truth of the Matter

Special Photographer for Public Relations with the CPR was no ordinary job. It included continuous traveling, moving equipment and baggage on a daily basis, with one of the largest CPR expense accounts to cover the costs of hiring people and renting equipment. Nick had freedom to work, but with that freedom came a great responsibility, and virtually no time off!

For years the Morants had no real home. Nick and Willie did not raise a family. That was their choice. Willie was a key partner not only in Nick's personal life, but in his job as well. It was only fair to her and to any children that a family was out of the question...

Willie became a key part in this thing, claims Nick, *and had we had a family, I would never have seen her, nor she me, nor would I have been seeing the family very much for that matter! Some undoubtedly would say that we were selfish... Maybe that's true, but that was the way it was, and we chose to go that way right or wrong. I sincerely believe that Willie was very happy in what she was doing.*

The Morant family, however, encompassed many young people. Their family included all their close friends and often their friends' children, as well as many outsiders that were welcomed into their home. The health and welfare of those they took an interest in was always foremost on their minds. You always felt, somehow, that you were returning home ... after that first tea.

Whenever friends or neighbors found their children in trouble, Nick and Willie were ready to help, and often made the difference between a successful life and that of a jailbird. They "Big Brothered" a lot of children...

There was Sam, and there was Rudolph, and little Lucette, simply kids whose parents neglected to find time to raise them, explained Nick.

Though it was much less prevalent in those days, some parents found it necessary for both to work to further themselves financially...

These people tended to neglect their children even when they weren't working. They'd go off on their own pleasures, leaving the kids to fend for themselves. I've seen several instances where burglaries were committed on our street directly the responsibility of those kids who had nobody even to give them a glass of milk or a cookie! So there were all of these young characters that we looked after for several and many years, all of whom I hear from at various times throughout the year, and one of them, Jamie Sanborn, would spend every holiday with me here in Banff.

The title "Special Photographer" sounds like an enviable one, a position that many would love to have, especially with an unlimited expense account!...

I was saying, explains Nick, *that one of the reasons why we have some successful shots here is that I always had an unlimited expense account and nobody ever questioned anything that I did. I had to make a shot once of a CPR policeman for the front cover of the old Spanner, and, knowing the CPR, a picture like that was likely being made at the order of the President, Mr.Neal. He had an idea we should run pictures of typical CPR workers. So I set out across the country to make a whole collection of photographs to be run on front covers for an entire year.*

When we came to making a picture of a CPR investigator, a policeman at work, we chose a guy who was a nice looking, kindly sort of chap, not the type who would come in and beat the living tar out of some kid who happened to be in a box car. So I decided to make the picture of him in a freight shed. We would use low lighting, underneath his chin to highlight his face, and we would have him looking around with a stern look on his countenance. Further, we thought, let's have the guy looking around some packing crates, only this time he's shining his flashlight up, and in the beam of light is a little kitten standing up there as cute as can be.

So now I had to get a kitten.

"Well, we got a cat down there at the freight shed, there's several of them!" someone pipes up.

Down we go to the freight shed and I explain that I'm from Public Relations in Montreal and we're down here doing some photographs for the Spanner.

"Well, certainly," says the chief clerk of the Winnipeg freight office, "we've got all kinds of pussycats down here!"

"How about Timmy?" somebody would say.

Well, Timmy would be fine, I said, let's have a look at him. Out we go to the freight shed, men rushing around with huge trolleys loaded with crates and whatnot.

The chief clerk hollers out, "Anybody seen Timmy around?"

Everyone stops. Somebody yells back, "Timmy just went down over there; you'll see him down in his regular spot."

So we went down to his regular spot, which was in a sort of coal hole beside the furnace where you could see under the floor boards. When I looked in there, just about at eye level was this cat, a great big Tom, who looked daggers at me -ferocious as hell!

Somebody tried to coax him out, but he just laced out with razor claws and left a three-inch scratch in the guy's hand. That was enough, I decided Timmy was not what I was looking for.

Well look, I said, let's not fool around. Now we had people looking who should be working. The chief clerk was there, the assistant chief clerk and others were all there, out to see the excitement. Nobody was getting anything done; I had disturbed the whole place.

So I said, Let's not fool around, I'd better go

and get a kitten at the Winnipeg Pet Shop. I'll come back, if I may, with the policeman again at one o'clock. We returned later with the kitten

You will note on July 15th, an item from the Winnipeg Pet Shop, rental of a kitten $.75.

I then went to work and said:

Doubtless somebody will inquire, quote, why wasn't a company cat used on this job?

I then proffered my excuse and went on to say that the first person to become involved with this affair was the chief clerk and gave his salary rate approximately, by the hour. And then the assistant chief clerk who came along to help - his salary. Then the foreman of the gang outside and several of his helpers. Pretty soon, I stated, we would have been faced with a payroll of one hundred dollars instead of 75 cents for the kitten.
The guy who made out the expense account begged me not to give this. "Just put it down to a bell-boy," he pleaded.
No way, I said, that's what I paid for the cat! It caused no end of amusement in the accounting office, but it was honest!

People, says Nick, *have no idea of the difficulties and trying circumstances surrounding what sounds like the world's greatest job. Despite the luxuries of eating meals in the great dining rooms of the Canadian Pacific chain of hotels, travelling gratis on all CPR lines and passenger trains, and sometimes ships and planes, despite having the freedom to do the job in any way best determined by yourself (you had the absolute confidence of the Public Relations Department since nobody was any the wiser), it was a strange and demanding career. In the 40 years I worked for the CPR, I think I can safely say I never took more than five holidays. I took only one holiday of any consequence and that was in 1967. With two days' notice Willie and I went over to England. We left all our stuff behind in the office and just sailed to England for six weeks.*

The job was such that Morant might not do a thing for weeks...
I might come into the office and pretend to look busy and finally the boss would say, "You'd better go out and do something!"
So I would go. Mostly I handled my own assignments as I made a point of keeping in touch with all the people concerned with Public Relations in the hotels, steamships and airlines, as well as the railway. If I was to be in their area for one job or another, I would contact everyone beforehand to see if there was anything needing attention.
A great deal of this work Morant did on his own time, but then his was not a nine-to-five, Monday to Friday job, nor were his duties distinct, but it was up to him to be of use to Public Relations, to justify his position and in the long term contribute to the earnings of the CPR through his part in promoting the Company. It is significant to note that upon his retirement, no one was appointed or hired to fill his job!
That the job took its toll on Nicholas Morant goes without saying. We must remember too, that Willie was there every step of the way. Behind these adventures, mishaps, and day to day tribulations, supporting all he did or tried to do, was Willie.
Morant's position in the Company and his ability to produce photographic material without failure caused constant strain. He was a perfectionist who actually reached a level of perfection that he was then expected to maintain. Morant always did things right... "Call Morant, he'll provide you with what you need."

People expected him to be able to handle any job because he had always done so...
That constant business of having to produce something without failure - there was no room for failure! The pressure was always on me. I would get quite distraught worrying about it at times.
Then in later years Willie became depressive, and it was a strange thing. Willie was always whistling around the house when one day I

noticed that she had quit. She never whistled again, ever!

Nick's devotion to Willie was especially evident in the years of her depression. Many miles were driven on weekends to visit her in hospital, and long hours spent on the road to return to work projects five hundred miles distant.
After many years of medical counselling, trauma and treatments, Willie again became herself. The years passed as Nick and Willie travelled the country on CPR business, and entertained guests and relatives in their home in Banff.
One day, long after Nick's official retirement from the CPR, the unexpected happened. On a quiet spring morning, on the living room couch, Willie was doing her needlepoint when she became faint and weak. Quick action and expert medical attention could do nothing, heart disease struck her down. It happened quickly and was fatal. Perhaps that was better than being bedridden or paralyzed, but we all miss her, none more so than Nick.

* * * * *

Willie and a friend. *NMC*

The turquoise pond nestled below the Beehive on the trail to Lake Agnes is called Mirror Lake. Willie and the packer that Morant hired, look out over the scene toward Lake Louise from the cliff on the right. Above them (from left to right) stands Mt. Victoria (11365'), Mt. Lefroy (11280') and Mt. Aberdeen (10350'). *NMC*

Portfolio IX

The Mountains

Skiing became a huge tourist attraction in the Banff area
after the 1950s. Even before that time however, Morant was
making ski photographs at Sunshine Village, Mt.Assiniboine
and the Skoki Lodge. *NMC*

A packer and his client who just happens to be Willie Morant, ride through the Sunshine meadows on the Great Divide. The mountain towering to the southwest is Mount Assiniboine (11870'). Nick and Willie made many trips with the "Trail Riders of the Canadian Rockies" and the "Skyline Hikers of the Rockies," all clients of the CPR. *NMC*

Morant's photographs often became the subject of stamps and Canadian bank notes. His photographs of Emerald Lake and Mt.Burgess (8473') decorated the ten dollar bill. Canadian Pacific had a lodge at Emerald Lake, seen in the lower right of the photograph, and the world famous Burgess shale fossil beds were exposed at the top of Burgess pass just behind the tree at left. *NMC*

High on the alpine meadows overlooking Hector Lake, with Mt. Balfour and the Balfour Glacier looming in the background, Willie sits with Jimmy Simpson, guide and packer, who stands behind her. The distinct color of the water is due to the glacial silt, like finely ground flour, that is carried directly into the lake from the hanging glacier. Mt. Balfour was named by Sir James Hector (after whom the lake is named), Surgeon and geologist to the Palliser Expedition of 1857 - 1860, in honour of John Hitton Balfour, M.D., founder of the Botanical Society of Edinburgh, professor of botany at Glasgow University and Dean of Medicine at the University of Edinburgh in 1859. NMC

This gentleman is fly fishing along the Bow River at Banff, Cascade Mountain (9836') is in the background, to the north. *NMC*

Fishing was a favourite pastime for Morant publicity photographs of the Canadian Rockies. These models were photographed at the Vermilion Lakes near Banff with the Sundance Range to the south. *NMC*

Way above Paradise Valley, Willie looks down toward
Paradise Creek and the Giant's Steps. Lake Annette nestles
below the ominous north face of Mount Temple (11636').
NMC

At the Giant's Steps, Willie watches the rushing water as it disappears into a chasm in the aptly named Paradise Valley. *NMC*

A Brewster Gray Line Courier Skyview descends Sunwapta Pass heading back to Banff with a load of enthralled sightseers. Directly above the bus is the ice capped peak of Mt.Athabasca (11452') with Parker's Ridge to the right. *NMC*

In one of Morant's most famous photographs, the Ten Peaks rise above Moraine Lake in the Valley of the Ten Peaks. This photograph, used to illustrate CPR advertisements, traveled the world in magazines and flyers and epitomized the Canadian Rockies. *NMC*

Mount Assiniboine, oft called the "Matterhorn of the Rockies" basks in alpen glow. Morant made the photograph from Erling Stroms' lodge on Magog Lake where he often went for skiing shots in the winter. *NMC*

A Moose feeds in the Vermilion Lakes near Banff at dusk. This was the time of day Morant often referred to as the magic hour, the time during and after sundown when the light became exquisite for photography. *NMC*

Fall in the Selkirk Mountains near Rogers Pass is a time when the native Huckleberries are ripe, and their leaves turn many hues of gold before the snows come. The great pyramid in the distance is Mt.Sir Donald (10818', originally named Syndicate Peak) and that is the Sir Donald Range that forms the wall at the east end of the Illecillewaet River valley. *NMC*

The golden Aspen trees along the Bow Valley forewarn
the coming of winter. It is September, probably the most
beautiful time in the Rockies, and that is the distinctive form
of Castle Mountain (9445') to the north. *NMC*

The missionary church at the Native reserve near Windermere looks west toward Mt.Nelson and the Purcell Mountains, what David Thompson named "Nelson's Mountains" upon receiving word of Horatio Nelson's triumph and death at Trafalgar. *NMC*

The Lanzo farm at Revelstoke, B.C. with Mt.Begbie (8985') rising more than 7000 feet above the Columbia River valley. *NMC*

A montage created for Morant's <u>Spanner</u> article relating ghost stories on the CPR. *NMC*

CHAPTER 14

Favorite Stories of a Photojournalist

Nick Morant has always been interested in the supernatural, though he is not a superstitious person...

There is something there, he claims, *when you talk about people with extra sensory perception.* In writing stories for the Spanner and CP Rail News in years past, Morant recorded some very strange happenings. Before their publication he made every effort to authenticate and verify the accuracy of the stories, separating hearsay and rumors from the actual events that took place. Only then were they exposed to his interested readers. Here follows then, a compendium of some of the more interesting accounts, all written by Morant with due thanks to CP Rail's employee publications...

The first is an article entitled.. <u>Close Encounters (... but not close enough)</u> by CP Rail News resident expert on the supernatural, Nicholas Morant... a look at two UFO sightings along the right-of-way...

Unidentified flying objects (UFO's) have not always enjoyed the privileged position they occupy in modern conversation. Sightings, indeed, have become commonplace.

It was different in 1947, when one clear autumn evening, a young trainman working a freight between Winnipeg and Brandon made a stop for coal and water at Portage la Prairie.

As he went about his train inspection, walking westward alongside the boxcars on the north side of the track, he spotted a giant, cigar-shaped object in the sky. It seemed bathed in bluish-green light and was proceeding - not at any great speed - from north to south.

The description differs somewhat from most sightings since in that the craft seemed to be directing a beam of light - of great intensity - earthward from what appeared to be a searchlight.

(The trainman specified that it was a clear evening. As any engineman or motorist knows,

in clear conditions one does not actually see a beam of light unless there is dust or misty conditions. I wonder if what he saw was a laser beam -unheard of by most people in 1947).

After permitting him a good look, the mysterious machine turned off first the lights in the circular windows around its circumference and then the searchlight. In the words of the trainman: "Then it simply became impossible to see - it vanished like a fade-out in the movies!"

Other members of the train crew were occupied with their tasks and did not witness the incident.

The young trainman rose through the ranks to become Superintendent Al Fryers at Moose Jaw. He has since retired but is still active in public service in that area.

Recalling the incident, Al says: "It could have been 300 feet long at a mile or 150 feet at three quarters of a mile. There was simply nothing to provide a third dimension - no buildings, no trees - no clue at all to coming up with an estimate of its' size."

There have been many cases where more than one man witnessed a UFO. Engineman Andy Staysko (now retired) of Lethbridge, Alberta, and his fireman were running late on Train No.8 near Antelope, Saskatchewan in 1947.

"All of a sudden there it was," relates Andy. "I called out to the fireman, he saw it too and was as bug-eyed as myself."

What they saw has since become the standard UFO sighted all over the world, an elongated cigar shaped craft, surrounded with a bluish light and bearing circular or oval windows.

The track swung into the lee of some hillocks and the mysterious vehicle was lost to sight. When they cleared the curve there was nothing to see. Andy put the UFO's length at 300 feet and added that the fireman agreed with that figure. But, as in the Al Fryers case, there was no way of making a measurement.

It is interesting that both these early

sightings took place in 1947.

The next account relates to the infamous bear accident in 1939, and is a story Nick Morant wrote regarding supernatural happenings on the CPR...

The dictionary describes supernatural as: "Something due to or manifesting some agency beyond the forces of nature."

There are some people who are gifted with psychic powers, call them `extra sensory perceptionists' if you wish. I knew such a person once upon a time. She was hardly the popular picture of a turbanned charlatan seated before the glass globe in a circus tent, backgrounded by signs of the zodiac.

She was a young woman of great charm and many abilities and worked with me at the Banff Springs Hotel for several seasons as a Public Relations assistant. She forecast the bear accident which overtook myself and the guide Christian Hasler and it was during the six months I was in and out of hospital that I had good cause to recall her warning.

Sometime after that, when I visited the lady in Toronto, she told me that she "felt" there was to be an accident, but she admitted that she never sensed that a bear was to be involved. Rather, she explained: "I assumed the logical accident on a trail would be getting kicked by a packhorse."

Andy Staysko, retired engineer from Lethbridge, whom I also mentioned earlier, has been involved in some extraordinary railroad stories. Whilst interviewing him, I discovered he has enjoyed, over the years, certain perceptive abilities which the rest of us are denied...

"I was engineer on the 3091 standing at Magrath, Alberta, in June, 1925, my conductor was Peter Johnson and we had just finished switching a few cars when he came up to the engine to see about our next move," explained Staysko.

(In those days there was one siding between

Magrath and Spring Coulee to the west. This was Bradshaw and the train orders showed it full of cars).

Johnson suggested to Andy they should go for the meet with the Cardston local passenger at Spring Coulee. Andy looked at his watch and figured they had an hour and 13 minutes. Normal running time then was 35 minutes.

"Something told me I'd best sit where we were at Magrath," he recalled.

"I said to the conductor:`Peter, if you fellas don't mind, I've a funny feeling we should stop where we are and wait on that passenger!'"

The conductor made it easy for him: "It's up to you my boy, we'll just back her off the main and wait!"

This they did, but the passenger never showed and, since it was not reported running late, Johnson set up his telephone and soon learned from the dispatcher that a small trestle over an irrigation canal had been underminded by a beaver and collapsed. Fortunately, the section gang had discovered it and flagged down the passenger train before it was due to cross.

Had Andy Staysko tried to run for the meet he might well have dumped his locomotive 18 feet into 12 feet of water.

"To this day," said Andy, "I don't know what got into me!" But he remembered the words of Fred Bryan, engineer on the passenger whilst talking with Superintendent C.D. McIntosh about the incident.

"Andy," said Fred, "if you live up to those hunches you should be alive a long time!"

On another occasion, Andy Staysko was engineer on a mixed train between Consul and Val Marie, Saskatchewan in 1934, with Fred Connolly firing. It was springtime and there was considerable run-off from the long winter's snow. At one point along the line he encountered a section crew with a track motor and asked the foreman if he'd been patrolling the area just recently.

When the answer was no, Andy's old ESP mechanism started ticking and again came the premonition of trouble. So he backed his train and let the section crew go ahead to 'pilot' them. Two and a half miles east of Frontier, on a slight curve, there were the section men frantically waving their arms like so many windmills. A badger had bored a hole beside a culvert and the spring run-off had undermined the entire fill. When Andy stopped his train he found the tracks hanging 13 feet off the ground for a distance of a full car length.

It is interesting to note that when engineer Andrew Staysko retired he had 65 merit marks to his credit, so it would appear this mysterious gift served him in good stead over the 48 years, 8 months he worked in railroading.

One of the most interesting stories Andrew Staysko had to tell was not a personal experience of his but an amazing story of some of the railroaders he knew early on in his career. This was also included in a series of articles Morant wrote for CP Rail News concerning strange occurrences along Canadian Pacific's right-of-way. As written by Morant, Staysko relates the story...

"This was a pleasant evening in June 1908. Engineer Bob Twohey and fireman Gus Day were taking their light engine up Dunmore Hill from the Medicine Hat roundhouse to relieve the engine and crew off the westbound Spokane Flyer.

"The connecting rods clanked quietly and the measured, almost contented sounds of the locomotive's exhaust alone disturbed the silence of the Alberta countryside. It was just before eleven o'clock.

"As they approached one of several blind curves along the track, which follows the side of a three-mile coulee, Twohey was startled by the sound of the whistle of another train. Then he was blinded by the sight of a glaring headlight of an approaching train and in the full knowledge that he was operating on single track, he reached for his controls but it was a hopeless gesture.

"With a roar the train was upon him and he was aware of the smoke over the cab of the engine turning red as its fireman opened the firebox door - a familiar enough sight in days of steam.

"Despite the fact he was on a single track, the next thing he recalled was that the nightmarish train was now passing him. Both men were to confide later with close friends that the passing `Phantom Train' had lights in the coaches, silhouetting the passengers inside them.

"More than that, the front end trainman and his conductor were in the vestibule to wave a friendly highball which, moments later, was repeated by the tail end man.

"As quickly as it takes to relate this, the Phantom Train had vanished. The experience left both men's brows glistening with sweat from the sheer terror of it. They continued their run, took over the Flyer on schedule and it was not until several days later, when the two men met off duty on the street in Medicine Hat, that they came to realize they both shared this frightening secret. With the exception of closest friends or relatives, they agreed not to share it with anyone. For who would have believed them?

"This was the era when Canadian Pacific Railway operated the Spokane Flyer, which ran from Spokane northwards to Yahk, B.C., through Cranbrook and the Crowsnest Pass to Lethbridge. Swinging south it bypassed Medicine Hat and joined the mainline at Dunmore Junction to continue on to Moose Jaw, then southwards into the United States, terminating in Chicago. Since the train did not go into Medicine Hat it was necessary to run relief engines and crews seven miles up the Dunmore Coulee to the junction. It must be recalled that in those days, crews as well as engines generally changed off at division points.

"Following the chance meeting with Gus Day on the street, Twohey became more and more alarmed and distraught over the incident. It preyed on his mind to such an extent that he visited a fortune teller. He received little encouragement. He was told he had less than a month to live. Then he made an attempt to strike back at Fate. He booked off work for a while.

"Shortly afterwards, fireman Day found himself assigned to the same locomotive on which he had travelled with Twohey when they encountered the Phantom Train. However, this time, the engineer was James Nicholson.

"Approaching the same bend in the track, they both heard the moan of a locomotive whistle. This was Day's second time but now Nicholson, who knew nothing whatever about the matter, was treated to the horrifying sight of the approaching glare of a headlight. Once again, the train passed them by, the forms of the passengers visible in their coaches and, again, the ghostly highballs from the train crew. In seconds the apparition was gone leaving those in the light engine speechless.

"Three men, one of them on two different occasions, had now seen the Phantom train at the same location, each time from the same locomotive. Was it some form of mass hallucination?

"It is unlikely there will ever be an explanation - but retired engineer Andy Staysko, alive and well at age 86 and still holding his driver's license in Lethbridge, knew Gus Day very well and shared an intimacy with him which extended for many years after the event.

"On the morning of July 8, Gus Day related to Staysko, he went to work at Medicine Hat and found himself assigned to yard duties. In his place on the light engine to relieve the westward Spokane Flyer that morning was Harry Thompson. The engineer was James Nicholson. Inexorably now, Fate was taking over and the Spectre of Death stood waiting at Privett's Brickyard crossing one mile away.

"In full daylight, the light engine was approaching the area of the Phantom Train. Not on a corner, however, but on a fairly long tangent (straight away) James Nicholson looked for the last time at an oncoming train.

"It was not an hallucination this time. The Crowsnest Local, Number 17, was running late.

"In the holocaust of steam and twisted metal that followed the head on collision, James Nicholson was fatally injured. Fireman Thompson was badly hurt in his jump to safety. The engineer of Number 17 was Robert Twohey, who tried so hard to beat Fate. He died in the wreckage with his fireman, in the searing inferno of live steam inside the cab of his overturned locomotive.

"The Medicine Hat News, July 9, 1908, headlined the `Awful Railway Wreck This Morning.' The next edition listed five railroaders killed along with two passengers in the telescoped wooden coaches of the era.

"At the inquests (there were two), questions were asked about the `clearance' given by operator Ritchie. It was the opinion of the jury that `he had failed to note on his clearance form

to engine 702 that train 17 had not yet arrived.' The jury also blamed Nicholson because he `failed to check the train register and ascertain for himself whether or not this clearance was correct.'

"There was evidence that operator Ritchie might have been physically exhausted at the time, but, though he was called to the inquest, he never testified.

"He vanished without a trace following the mishap and was never found, in spite of extensive searches by the Royal North West Mounted Police.

"Surely Fate blindfolded these men. Could three of them forget a Time Card train? Of Nicholson there was a suggestion that he had encountered family problems the morning of his departure that might have taken his mind off his work - if for only a few fatal seconds.

"Cause of Nicholson's death, as specified legally, was shock. And who can wonder at that?

The headline story of the <u>Vancouver Province</u> on August 9, 1925 read: "Only Miracle Saved Kettle Valley Express From Destruction." Further to the strange occurrences that have happened from time to time along the CPR, Nick Morant wrote a piece for <u>CP Rail News</u> in 1977 entitled; "Phantom Signaller Sounded Warning," which we have here reproduced...

The story had been picked up from the <u>Toronto Star,</u> then, as now, prone to the sensational touch. The Star writer related:

"It was seven miles east of North Bend, B.C., and the long train of human freight was gathering speed every foot of the way as she roared along the pathway of double steel ribbons, flashing silver-like in the powerful rays of the big electric headlight. The fireman, his brow glistening with sweat, was bent to his task while the silent engineer, like the driver of a racing motor car peering down the speedway, looked constantly into the pitch black night, cut only by the single blue-white shaft shooting from the front of the steaming monster locomotive."

But, Morant discovered, it wasn't the Kettle Valley Express, it was train No.1, the famous Trans-Canada Limited. Also the

events that followed occurred about seven or eight miles east of Spence's Bridge...

In researching the past, writers are often faced with the problem of finding the truth, which is frequently more exciting reading than a cooked up version relying, as in many cases, on picturesque language. It means sifting out the fiction deliberately used to 'color the yarn' by a well meaning author, as well as detecting untruths arising from honest misunderstandings.

The story related here is true and was attested to in Canadian Pacific's Vancouver records. Through the assistance of L.R.Smith, Senior Regional Vice-President, and that of N.A.Sewell, his Superintendent of the Canyon Division, I came to correspond with an old friend, Lloyd Snowden, of Kamloops, B.C., currently involved with the Engineman's Training Project.

I shall spare readers colorful descriptions of passenger trains screeching around curves in the gorges of the Fraser River Canyon; instead I present an un-edited version of the letter written by Lloyd Snowden, who was then running Kamloops to North Bend on regular passenger service. The letter reads:

"I enclose a copy of the newspaper story of the incident which appeared in the <u>Vancouver Province.</u> As usual a newspaper rarely ever reports anything accurately and this one is certainly no exception as indicated by the information given me some years later by my father (W.R.Snowden) as to what actually happened that night of December 31, 1924.

"As I remember, my father was ordered at Kamloops for the night passenger west and at the time it was very cold, about 20 degrees below zero. As he told me, the train was a bit late and he was making up time so as to be in North Bend on the dot.

"Upon reaching Toketic, which was located in those days at mileage 67.3, he received two distinct whistles on the communicating signal appliance while going through the reverse curves east of that station.

"The siding at Toketic at that time had a capacity of 57 cars and the stop was made with the engine about 15 car lengths west of the west switch. The conductor walked up to the engine on the north side of the train and denied giving the signal to stop, upon which, he gave the signal to proceed."

Here I interject to describe what happened next, because my good friend, Lloyd Snowden, unlike myself, has been trained to make plain statements of fact - a trait that all running trades-men will understand only too well.

Bill Snowden started the train and, as the headlight swung around, he and his fireman were astonished to see a locomotive standing a few hundred yards down the mainline -showing no lights, shrouded in its own steam in the sub zero night!

But let Lloyd continue...

"The engineer and fireman were found to be asleep in their cab. It was evident to my father the brakes on the other engine were released and that the main throttle was leaking badly.

"The crew on the engine had worked all day and into the night on a work train between Spence's Bridge and Merritt (a branch line to the south). After taking coal and water at `The Bridge' on the main track, the locomotive was backed into the house track where the men fell asleep while waiting for the passenger train. My father told me that the engineer had probably placed the reverse lever in the forward position so as to be more comfortable on the seat. The fireman had banked the fire and with the main throttle leaking sufficiently to close the relief valves, the subsequent pressure build-up of steam in the cylinders moved the engine gently out of the house track and through the main track switch.

"The engine coasted eastwards from Spence's Bridge to just east of milepost 68.0 where it was found - a distance of approximately seven miles.

"Somewhere short of this point, the steam pressure being quite low, the relief valves opened and the engine moved slowly down the slight grade and stopped at the bottom of the sag.

"Some railroaders believed that the air hose connections between the passenger cars on Dad's train, due to sub zero conditions became very stiff and the fast movement of the train on the

reverse curves caused sufficient leakage at the hose gaskets to cause the signal to blow in the cab.

"Conversation between the conductor and my father upon arrival at North Bend, revealed the vestibule door on the first day coach behind the baggage car, south side of the train, was open, but this was not known until after the train left Spence's Bridge. The open door was not discovered by the conductor at Toketic because he got off at the other end of the coach and walked to the engine on the opposite side.

"Although the trap over the steps was down, it was thought someone might have opened the door and jumped off when the stop was made at Toketic. However, the conductor said all passengers were accounted for and nobody appeared missing.

"The strange sounding of the signal to stop, which was clearly heard by the fireman and my father in the cab on that cold winter's night will forever remain a mystery. You can be sure, if the train had not received the signal at that particular time and proper action had not been taken immediately, there would have been a disastrous collision."

Disastrous collision, indeed, wrote Morant. The tracks stand close to the fast running Thompson River and on a fairly steep embankment. But what did we have here? An act of the supernatural? A faulty gasket or some other mechanical failure? Whatever - how do we account for the simultaneous sounding of the signal with the presence of a lone engine standing on the main line? Is there indeed a Watcher over us?

* * * * *

In his articles for CP Rail News and the Spanner, Morant wrote many stories of people along the line, the employees who kept the railroad running. Many of the work trains and extra gangs have cook cars on them to feed the hard working men and keep them on their work locations as they maintain the railway. In one particular article, Morant wrote an amusing story entitled: "Our Hazel - The Nemesis of Furry Cake Pilferers." It went as follows...

The boys on extra gangs around Revelstoke and Kamloops accept Mrs.Hazel Beveridge for what she is; a darned good cook and a kindly grandmother given to smoking the odd cigar. This is one side of her character.

A dangerous looking female, wielding a threatening broom is the other side of Mrs.Beveridge and this is the awe inspiring sight which meets the eyes of black bears who intrude upon the privacy of her cook car.

A few weeks ago she caught one sitting at a table in the deserted dining area. He was knocking off a few of her banana cakes with obvious relish such as to cause a surge of pride in any other chef. Not true in this case. Three resounding whacks on the bear end and Brother Bruin was glad to see the last of Hazel Beveridge, who had to substitute canned pears for dessert that night.

Less than three weeks later, another bear in a different district, took revenge for the shameful rout she had accorded one of his distant cousins. Moaned Hazel, to those who would listen, `This one caught me asleep. Five cakes, four raisin pies and a whole bunch of broken dishes and I never got in one whack at the black...!' One word deleted here since it is of slanderous nature suggesting his parents were unmarried.

* * * * *

"Folks - meet the Rogers Camp Bearcat!" began another of Morant's articles for CP Rail News. Rogers Camp was the pusher engine terminal for the Beaver Hill on CPR's main line through the Roger's Pass. Locomotive and maintenance crews lived in this isolated camp until 1989 when the new "MacDonald" tunnel eliminated the need for pusher engines on westbound trains. In a rather hilarious animal story, Morant recounts the exploits of one feline resident of that camp that, we are told, is far more than just a "tall tale!"...

Now before we go any further into this feline phenomenon, editors of CP Rail News questioned me sternly and demanded to know how much more of this wild stuff readers could be expected to stomach? There have been ghost trains, mysterious hands pulling communications cords, not to mention one about *a little old lady who smokes cigars and chases bears with a broom.*

So I have Dave Williams of Revelstoke, not only to thank for this story of `Rags' but also for a list of nearly a dozen witnesses to the madcap antics of the aggressive pussycat.

`Rags,' sometimes known as `Mommy' for obvious reasons, joined the Rogers Camp two years ago and her progeny now populate other camps along the line, handling considerable traffic themselves as they swiftly dispatch pilfering rodents. Mommy, when she is caring for a new litter of kittens, tends to get somewhat skittish if bears start nosing around camp, and that's putting it mildly.

Williams has an eyewitness account of what usually happens if Mommy decides to send one of these black intruders on his way. It is a terrifying affair. "At sight of the bear she bristles out her fur to twice normal size. She snarls a number of warnings and then takes a running leap upon the back of the bear, just forward of his shoulders, rodeo rides him, literally, off the property and back into remote areas of the surrounding forest." (There's more, you may wish to give your kids parental guidance here because what follows is violence for cat's sakes.) Let Williams continue...

"She clamps her sharp teeth into the bear's scalp, spurring his neck with her rear claws spinning like buzzsaws. She stabs at his ears with her front claws, cowboy style as it were, steering the panicked bruin among pusher engines, parked vehicles and section men running for their lives.

"Whilst all this is going on, she rotates her tail like a helicopter, apparently developing aerodynamic thrust. The resulting uproar can be compared to a set of bagpipes going through a clothes dryer."

Fooling aside, the cat does indeed attack bears and has done so on a number of occasions in just the manner described here.

Witnesses you say? Camp manager Keith Parson, cooks Mr. and Mrs.Joe Adam, section foreman Steve Redly and one of his men, Randy Murphy. Then there's pusher enginemen Rex Jones, Bob Wilford and Bobby Bruce, and east end hogger Kip Holloway; Pearse Gilmour, signal maintainer and his helper Derek Lane.

And then, of course, there's a couple of disgruntled bears!

* * * * *

On assignment for the CPR in 1952, Nick and Willie travelled in a caboose to a siding called Jessica, on the Coquihalla Subdivision of the railway in the Cascade Mountains east of Vancouver. There the caboose was set out into a back track, and they lived there for about three weeks.

Nick was sent in to photograph this extremely scenic line and the passenger trains that traversed it. A schedule change had been instituted to try to attract more patronage across this route, and the company wanted to tout the scenic wonders to be seen on the daylight run.

Nick discovered that there were quite a number of characters who just simply lived there, just how, no one was sure. There were some who were ex-convicts and some who were just plain hermits and others who maintained the railway through the pass. In a letter to Montreal friend Colin Haworth, Morant humorously described some of those people:

It so happens I am, at the moment, writing this in a caboose in the Coquihalla Pass in southern B.C. The weather has been bad and I have, for once, had a little time to myself - away from the drudgery of lecturing, building a house and working for the Canadian Pacific RR...

The Coquihalla Pass - HERE you can get away from it all. Well - almost. There ARE people around. Gunnar Heistadt, section foreman at Jessica, had a bad time a few nights ago -his dead father and mother visited him in his house. Gunnar was quite drunk, somewhat upset and so was his cat - they all came yelling bloody murder out of the back door together. Gunnar, in fact, occasionally pierces the inky black silence of the nights when he has had a few too many rums. I understand, in the big cities, that the psychiatrists call it delirium tremens - or is that what they put in Chipso now and call it Dreft?

Gunnar has friends. Or shall we term them riders? Anyway three of them, Gunnar being at the helm at the time, went over a mild sort of

precipice in their track motor. Gunnar was three months in hospital; the CPR official report, I'm told off the record, would indicate that there was a high percentage of rock deposited on the main track and it was fortunate indeed that Gunnar and his friends hit this instead of the passenger train that night. But, of course, the passenger train does not come up from Hope (and the beer parlors) at 3.00 a.m. with the engineer singing quaintly old Swedish ballads - with no headlight on. Everybody else is scared to death of the Coquihalla Pass, its multitudinous trestles and bottomless chasms - but not Gunnar... but then, lets have a few words with Gunnar himself, about the time he met the work train with fifteen cars of gravel coming backwards around a curve, just as Gunnar is going forwards, and meeting this awe inspiring sight in a narrow cutting.

"Jeziss, bichris, I stop de god damnut yalopy wit a yolt... son of a beech is gone into me so I yump off and signal like hell but ain't nobody to see me - engineer ain't lookin,' f____n fireman is making tea and yust no one about. Sheet you know its haffa mile before they find my speeder underneath a carload of gravel - but it ain't damaged moch... just a viggle in her now."

This by way of explaining to me how it was the damned front axle is bent - forty miles an hour over two hundred foot trestles all day long on a speeder with a bent axle.

And then there is Gentle Alex. He lives three hundred feet below the tracks and the only clue to Alex (nobody can pronounce his last name except the Warden at New Westminster) is a weird windlass device which stands beside the right of way. Alex fancies himself as the Thomas A. Edison of the lower Coquihalla area. He signs all his mail - and his income tax return, 'Inventor.' The windlass stands, as I said, beside the tracks and at the head of a 30 degree runway, tracked with logs parallel to one another on which travels a sort of sleigh with greased runners. Alex refuses to let himself down on this runway but he does let his groceries down on it. Mostly this works very well, but last fall the cable broke and three hundred pounds of assorted and fancy groceries went plummeting down the chute, easily cleared a safety device near the bottom and neatly deposited the works into fifteen feet of water in the Coquihalla River. A great deal was recovered by the wily fellow who, as a full time inventor devised a dipper on a long handle with which he scooped out some of the canned stuff. This was fine and 100% recovery - except the element of surprise was injected into all his meals for the remainder of the winter - the labels were all washed off the cans. Full recovery was not made, however, in the case of the flour, sugar and certain breakfast cereals. Poor Alex is also troubled with bears - of whom he is, for some reason, deathly afraid. For instance, he was observed by a section man at dusk, who later reported to the neighborhood, that he was seen stalking a water barrel on a small trestle in mistake for a sitting bear. The barrel was dripping water in three great wounds when Alex was finished firing - but the payoff was that the bear which Alex had originally been stalking had reappeared from behind him and was watching, twenty feet from the section man, to see how good a shot this hunter really was. Apparently he was quite impressed with the bleeding barrel and beat a hasty retreat in the direction of the nearest National Park. Alex's biggest problem is transportation - this is a tough nut to crack such as to tax the imagination of Thomas A. or Robert Fulton. Living not only at the bottom of a steep canyon but also about three miles from the nearest stop made by trains - he must not only get the groceries down the side of the mountain - he must also transport them to the windlass. So, little wonder, Alex recently (and to nobody's surprise but his) met a freight train on a long trestle - there were lots of safety spots for Alex on the trestle but not for the two wheeled, rubber tired, oversize wheelbarrow he had invented which looks like a Montreal push-cart but built to Canadian Pacific's standard gauge track measurement. Where else would you push a goddam pushcart around here but on the track, you silly bastards? The engineer made a successful stop, wasn't too surprised to find Alex walking out his invention on the right of way and gave him a minute or so to do a rapid retreat back up the trestle and once again the railway settled down to do its day's business - with Alex off the right of way.

Alex is very sad - the Coquihalla River, beside which he lives, simply teems with steelhead. Alex with all his inventive genius has to admit complete failure in this direction, to the Japanese foreman here (Romeo, B.C.) he once said, hopelessly, "Someday, Bobby, (which is a helluva funny name for a Jap, but that's his name) will you please show me how to catch a fish - they won't bite at my hooks ever." Everyone, at this writing, particularly engineers who must pilot diesels across long trestles, is a bit concerned about Alex. Alex has bought a small 1926 truck - and the nearest known highway is 46 miles away - this could leave the right of way of the Canadian Pacific RR as a somewhat rough but nevertheless effective substitute - or at least in Alex's eyes anyway.

That Japanese section foreman - I used to go to his shanty at eight o'clock in the morning to get the dispatcher's lineup, and there he would be, sitting there taking the lineup, dressed in the most beautiful Japanese kimono you ever saw, hand decorated in the form of a dragon. He would be sitting there with one ear on one of those old beat up ear phones, smoking a cigarette in a long holder, knocking his ashes into a sardine can ashtray, all decked out in his kimono. A very courteous man, he was a very proud, haughty Japanese fellow.

There are others: Mr.McIntyre - the French Canadian who is running a small logging outfit and whose daughter has been trying to seduce one of the loggers in the outfit. Daughter, who is not only a cute little trick but is hep to most everything in life, was sitting in the kitchen a few nights ago when a bloody great rock came rolling down the embankment into their kitchen - via the only obvious means of entry, through the kitchen window. Yes, kiddies, it was her big bad father, Mr.McIntyre the French Canadian (he is so a French Canadian). He explained later he thought she was talking to the boyfriend.

Another time, dear daughter was around the place, when a government inspector thought to walk in unannounced to see what sort of a logging deal McIntyre was running and if he was operating according to law.

He saw the girl and foolishly said, "Hello - I'm lost -could you tell me where I am."

'Inspector' was written all over the bugger's face, I suppose, for she instantly replied, "This is Santa's hideout" and went in and closed the door. The story came from the wife of the telegraph lineman who had to feed the guy - he hadn't even brought his lunch!

P.S. I met Alex a few evenings ago as I was walking back along the track - alone - miles from anywhere. Alex had a rifle and there I was unarmed not too far distant from a water barrel on a trestle. Boy, did I whistle sweet tunes -not even Alex would shoot at an inoffensive water barrel with two legs, packing a tripod and who said good evening to him. Apparently Alex didn't trust me and my tripod either -because after we had passed one another I kept glancing back over my shoulder to make sure the sonofabitch hadn't stopped to take a bead on my retreating figure. Whaddya know? Everytime I looked back, there was poor Alex glancing back over HIS shoulder in just as apprehensive a manner. I'll bet both of us read TRUE DETECTIVE.

P.P.S. I almost forgot to tell you about Alex and the 60 loaves... Alex had an idea that you could buy an entire winter's supply of bread, tear off the wax wrappers and dry them in the sun and this would dehydrate them and they wouldn't go mouldy. So he set out all 60 loaves to dry in the sun and then went off for the day. When he came back the loaves had all vanished - which is another reason why at the drop of a water bucket Alex is inclined to fire at anything that looks like a bear.

Most everything that Alex has he has stolen and some of his cronies in the district live likewise. Some time ago one or two of them were up in arms... ALEX HAD STOLEN FROM THEM. Righteously they went to the cops and the upshot was Alex went to gaol. During which time there his pals moved in and swiped everything of Alex's - including his window frames. Offsetting this bitter pill was one thing, if we are to believe what Alex said, "Mrs.Phillips," (telegraph lineman's wife) he said, "the warden didn't want me to leave New Westminster (pen) - he said my ideas and inventions were too good to lose me."

By far the most interesting people at

Jessica were Mr. and Mrs. Phillips - the telegraph lineman and his wife. His job was to cover the whole area from Hope up to the top of the pass in all kinds of weather. Describes Morant...

Where the wires spanned a canyon like at Ladner Creek he had to go out there on a sort of 'bosun's chair' type of contraption and when he came to one of the catenary crossarms, he'd have to get out of the chair and lift it around the crossarms, climb over and get back in it to reach the next set of suspended crossarms. He had to hang on to it as he clambered around the crossarms because if he let go it would trundle out to the low part of the dip in the wires -out into space over a creek or canyon.

For many years Phillips did the job on his own, but later on as the company became more safety conscious they gave him an assistant. Apparently one of those assistants went out on the wires and froze from fear over a canyon. It was some rescue to get him out of his predicament - but that was the last of him in those parts!

Phillips died, it is said, slumped at the base of a telegraph pole while on the job, just prior to his retirement.

Bill Phillips was married to a most unusual woman known as the "Angel of the Coquihalla." Nick and Willie went and visited them whenever they were invited. The Phillips' had a comfortable little house, but what was amazing was scattered around the living room, on tables and in racks, were every cultural magazine you could ever imagine! The New Yorker, the Illustrated London News, the Field Magazine, which was a British country gentleman's magazine, and many others. Mrs. Phillips picked endless quantities of berries, a boundless resource during summer along the Coquihalla, and put up the most delicious huckleberry, raspberry, blackberry and wild strawberry jams, preserves - and pies! She would cool the pies on the window ledge of her kitchen - and you could smell the pleasant aroma for some distance around. Anyone who came to her house couldn't leave without

Bill Phillips, CPR lineman in the Coquihalla Canyon, replaces insulators on a hanging section of wires in the fall of 1953. Note the trapeze he used to reach this very precarious location. *NMC*

preserves, jam or pie, especially the section men who were batching up there. It was they who named her the "Angel of the Coquihalla." She and Willie Morant became great friends and corresponded for years.

But what a crazy mixed up bunch up there thought Morant, though, says Nick...

There never was any rough stuff around the place as it turned out. No one ever bothered anyone else.

* * * * *

So we see that, as well as fulfilling the responsibilities of Special Photographer for Canadian Pacific Public Relations, Morant took it upon himself to supply the company's employee publications not only with photographs for covers and articles, but with entertaining writing as well. When in school in Victoria, Morant wrote for the student newspaper; when growing up in Kamloops he attempted writing news articles; with the CPR in Winnipeg he wrote advertising brochures; with the <u>Winnipeg Free Press</u> he was a columnist as well as a news photographer; and finally with the CPR he became a frequent journalist for the <u>Spanner</u> and later <u>CP Rail News.</u> And so life has in this way come full circle for Morant. As a meticulous and inspirational photographer he found his profession, but in writing he found a passion for words well expressed, a prime interest since school days.

In this way Morant's photographs and words pervaded the <u>Spanner</u> and <u>CP Rail News</u> so that all CPR employees became well acquainted with the man and his name. Morant showed great interest in the railroad's employees, their jobs and hobbies, and their stories. As a result, the pages of CPR publications were filled with a wealth of interesting stories of employees and tales from along the line. He fully believed in the importance of company magazines or newspapers for the employees. He believed they were a large part of company morale and did nothing but promote the interests of the CPR amongst the people who ran the railroad.

Morant endeared himself to the employees through his interest in their lives. That was the kind of man he was. Full of concern for the lives of others - and that was true of Willie as well, Morant's "Girl Friday."

Willie herself claimed that nothing was more exciting or satisfying than becoming involved in her husband's career. She was quite caught up in the life that they led and the people they met. People were also caught up by her personality, especially so Nick, and there is no doubt that she was a prime factor in Morant's success.

This life they led meant hopping on a train at a moment's notice, climbing a mountain, or perhaps sitting motionless for three days beside a stream waiting for the optimum moment, the perfect light. The conventional hat-box and wardrobe case considered indispensable by most women was replaced by 55 bags and boxes of assorted size and weight containing all the paraphernalia dear to a photographer's heart, including a portable dark room!

Willie became a respected photographer herself over the years, and as chief advisor to Morant was responsible for many of the details surrounding the production of material for the CPR. She did everything from setting up equipment, arranging backgrounds for interior shots, supervising models and their costumes, to acting as backup photographer.

Because weather was so much a factor in their lives, routine hours became meaningless - hours and hours were spent trying to capture the perfect photographs, requiring patience and lots of it. But it was a most rewarding life and career for the two of them, and a measure of their lives can be made by the number of friends, acquaintances and admirers they have throughout Canada and the world.

In retirement, the Morants remained close to home, enjoying quieter moments than they often knew while employed by the railway. Friends and acquaintances were always dropping by and the tea kettle was always on. Morant still had time for stories, the experiences of his life providing ample subject matter. On quiet evenings with no other audience than the denizens of his backyard, Morant might entertain himself with a flute recital, playing along with a taped orchestra, strictly for his own enjoyment and relaxation...

One evening after cleaning the instrument, relates Morant, *I was listening to some unfamiliar music, attempting to tune my flute to it so that I could play along. As I was playing the instrument, I just caught this slight movement out of the corner of my eye, and there's this little fellow looking up at me with big eyes and little ears all perked up. So I stopped playing and started a conversation with him.*

"Did you fall down the chimney? You know you've got to get out, away you go!"

I quietly walked over and confronted him. I could have swatted him I guess, but he just looked up at me with those big eyes as if he had no one else to turn to. I started to try to do something. I got the wastepaper basket and dropped it on top of him. He didn't like that! He left in a great hurry before I could get him. He was all over the room! He was everywhere!

He climbed up the drapes and then took off, as flying squirrels do from a tree branch, gliding hither and thither. He would disappear for a moment then come back into sight and just stare at me. Finally, I was able to move so that he was cornered into leaving by one of the doors I had opened. He seemed reluctant to leave, however, as I guess he was quite comfortable in the house. They are, in fact, very docile creatures!

* * * * *

The Morant's backyard with Willie at the back door. Nick is behind the camera that is camouflaged by the woodpile that he built just for such photographic opportunities. *NMC*

A drill rig at Lake MacGregor in southern Alberta works into the night, circa 1973. *NMC*

Portfolio X

Canadian Pacific Oil and Gas

In the Leduc fields near Edmonton, drill rigs explore
the dimensions of Canada's most famous discovery, circa
1947. *NMC*

The derrickman, chainman and floorman, spattered in mud, prepare to add another stand of pipe as the driller, in back, maneuvers the controls of the headblock, on the floor of a drill rig somewhere in western Canada. *NMC*

Under a clear sky and a bright moon, a light weight exploration rig works in the boreal forests of the Northwest Territories searching for oil or gas. *CPCA*

At the foot of the Rockies, on a clear fall day in
southern Alberta, a big rig called a "triple" drills deep into
the sediments in the search for new petroleum prospects.
CPCA

Epilogue

Nicholas Morant is congratulated by the Governor General of Canada, the Right Honourable Ray Hnatyshyn, at Government House in Ottawa, on the occasion of investiture into the Order of Canada on October 24, 1990. Photo by Government House Photographer Bertrand Thibeault.

Nick Morant, despite his scholastic standing at University School in Victoria those many years ago, had a way with words - his one winning subject. This he came by honestly through his poetess mother who had an elegant command of the English language. One day while Nick was growing up in Kamloops, he can remember when a particularly annoying woman announced to Mollie that she was going to visit her son in the sanitarium at Tranquille (near Kamloops), Mollie was heard to remark: "I should view her remaining there with composure."

Morant finally retired from the railway in 1980. Well, he didn't really retire - just began making photographs that he wanted to make - not that he had done anything else over the previous 40 years with the CPR. In retirement, he obliged the company with help in a number of PR projects, and stood from time to time, for lectures and interviews. Depending on the nature of the request, he would gear himself up to say something, but once on a roll, he is full of interesting stories and experiences.

One day he received a request from a gentleman representing the National Art Gallery in Ottawa for a major exhibition of Morant's work featuring 16 select negatives of Canada's grandeur, each enlarged to at least 20 feet in dimension! Such enlargements are not out of the ordinary these days, with fine grain film and modern processing techniques, and are ofen produced for advertising.

A good many of Morant's photos have been enlarged to wall size on occasion, and many four or five feet in width grace the walls of CPR railway stations and offices, as well as at travel agents in North America and Europe. But of course, such enlargements are expensive, and it was flattering for Morant to think that the

National Art Gallery was willing to invest so much in a show of his work.

As it turned out, the gentleman from Ottawa wanted Nick to supply the prints himself! The glory of the project faded suddenly after that, and was never done.

Meanwhile, Nick's voluminous negative file is up to date and in fine order, and he would add to it on occasion until just a few years ago. He has mumbled to people close to him that he ought to burn the lot for all the trouble they are, but that is his way of humorously getting a rise out of those who know the value of his material as an historically important collection of Canadiana.

This book gives a smattering of that collection, most of the photographs drawn from there, with the exception of some material from Canadian Pacific Corporate Archives.

Perhaps the most satisfying public recognition his work received was when Nick was awarded the Order of Canada in October, 1990. He was pleased, naturally, but his character set limits on his expression of enthusiasm. For Nick, a plain dark suit with a conservative tie was proper for him at the Investiture, rather than the dinner jacket, or tuxedo, that many wore. It was alright for his wife to dress up because "that's what women do," but for Nick his tuxedo days were long gone. Casual, but natty, comfort was now of more importance than trying to impress anyone.

To friends watching the ceremony on television, Morant performed well. When the Governor General made reference to "Morant's Curve" in his speech, it elicited a slight smile on Nick's countenance. Presented with the medal, he bowed respectfully to the Governor General, then moved to the side of the chamber, berating himself for not offering equivalent

acknowledgment to the Governor General's wife! The perfectionist in him demanded penance for a mistake that no one else had noticed. But that was the way of Morant.

It was no surprise to acquaintances that the Morants had travelled to Ottawa by train even though it was a devious proposition since government rationalization of passenger service had eliminated travel via the CPR. Still and all, the ceremony in Ottawa was at least a form of acknowledgment that this country is physically unmatched in its splendour, as this book attests.

Though admittedly, on a declining level of activity, Morant kept busy into his eighties with his own photographic interests and the publication of books marking his career and life. As people-oriented as he is, his life as a widower was not very fulfilling, so in January of 1990, he married again. Elizabeth Thomson of Calgary, widow of the late Rev. Arthur James Thomson, a cultured and delightful lady, became Mrs.Nicholas Morant. As one of Nick's close friends remarked, "Morant, always the perfectionist."

Betty stood especially proud in the audience at Rideau Hall on the night of October 24th, 1990, when Nicholas Morant was invested as a Member of the Order of Canada. She knew that this country needed to recognize Nick's work after all that he had done to give shape and image to the evolution of the nation from a Dominion to a mature world power.

Louis Jaques, the crusty, unbeatable dark-room man from Nick's old days on the National Film Board, wired a congratulatory message: "It's great to have at least one other Canadian photographer recognized." He was referring to Yousuf

Karsh, Canada's world-renowned portrait photographer who had previously been named to the Order of Canada. Few photographers have been so honored in this nation

* * * * *

Nick and Betty peruse a copy of <u>Nicholas Morant's Canadian Pacific</u> at their Banff home in 1992. Photo by Banff Crag and Canyon photographer Clint Reece.

The End